Loving and Beloved
Tales of Rabbi Levi Yitzhak of Berdichev, Defender of Israel

MENORAH

Simcha Raz

LOVING AND BELOVED

Tales of Rabbi Levi Yitzhak of Berdichev, Defender of Israel

TRANSLATED BY

Dov Peretz Elkins

Menorah Books

Loving and Beloved
Tales of Rabbi Levi Yitzhak of Berdichev,
Defender of Israel

First English Edition, 2016

Menorah Books
An imprint of Koren Publishers Jerusalem Ltd.

POB 8531, New Milford, CT 06776-8531, USA
& POB 4044, Jerusalem 9104001, Israel
www.korenpub.com

Original Hebrew Edition © Simcha Raz, 2008
English Translation © Dov Peretz Elkins, 2016

The publication of this book was made possible
through the generous support of *Torah Education in Israel*.

ISBN 978-1-59264-473-5, *hardcover*

A CIP catalogue record for this title is
available from the British Library.

Printed and bound in the United States

In loving memory of

Rabbi Aaron Landes, ז"ל

scholar, teacher, rabbi, admiral, husband,
father, grandfather, and friend

Who may ascend the mountain of the Lord?
Who may stand in His holy place?
He who has clean hands and a pure heart …
He shall receive a blessing from the Lord.
(Ps. 24:3–5)

Dedicated by
his student Rabbi Dov Peretz Elkins
and his son Joshua Landes

Contents

Translator's Preface

I am delighted and honored to have a part in bringing this book to the English-reading world.

First, because of my deep respect and admiration for my friend and teacher, Simcha Raz, a distinguished Israeli scholar and writer. This is the fifth book, originally written in Hebrew by Simcha Raz, that I have been privileged to publish in English. All five books are the product of Simcha Raz's lifelong study of the sacred literature of the Jewish people.

Simcha Raz has the unique ability to gather profound teachings from many places and imbue the sweetness and beauty of Jewish wisdom into a series of outstanding collections on many themes.

I particularly enjoyed translating this collection of tales of Rabbi Levi Yitzhak of Berdichev. The stories reflect the powerful ideology of one of the best-known hasidic masters, and the deep moral and spiritual heritage which he has bequeathed to future generations. Rabbi Levi Yitzhak's profound love of the Jewish people, his devotion to his Creator, and his powerful defense of all Jews – all of which earned him the title "Defender of Israel" – make him a model for the Jewish people of this century.

I want to thank those who assisted in making this translation smooth and accurate: Sahar Tzur, Yocheved Klausner, and my son Jonathan Elkins.

I am extremely grateful to my cherished friend, Joshua Landes, who encouraged and supported the publication of this special collection. Most appropriately this book is dedicated to the memory of his beloved and distinguished father, Rabbi Aaron Landes *z"l*.

I am also very grateful to Matthew Miller and the many people at Menorah Books who have shepherded this book to completion, especially editor Gila Fine. Thanks to the gifted staff at Menorah: Tomi Mager, Shira Koppel, Nechama Unterman, and Mia Hamburger. May the efforts of all these talented and industrious people help bring inspiration and enlightenment to all who are privileged to be influenced by the special stories of Rabbi Levi Yitzhak.

In closing, I want to thank my devoted wife, Maxine (Miryam), who tolerated my obsession with the computer during our first year after making *aliya*. Editing and translating this amazing book has brought me great joy and renewed appreciation of the Jewish tradition to which we have together devoted our lives.

Rabbi Dov Peretz Elkins
Rosh Ḥodesh Elul, 5776

Introduction

Rabbi Levi Yitzhak of Berdichev was born in 1740 in the village of Hosakov, Galicia (Poland). His father was Rabbi Meir, a descendant of a line of esteemed rabbis. At age twelve, he went to study Torah in a yeshiva in the city of Yaroslav. At age seventeen, he married the daughter of philanthropist Yisrael Peretz, a wealthy Jew of the city of Lebartov, who excelled in love of Torah and supported many poor young scholars.

The city of Lebartov was known as "Little Jerusalem," because of the many students living there. Rabbi Levi Yitzhak lived in Lebartov for several years studying Torah, and became a beloved friend of several great teachers. He grew close to Rabbi Shmelke Horowitz of Nikolsburg, and was a student of Rabbi Dov Ber, the Maggid of Mezritch, with whom he studied a great deal of Torah and Hasidism. He often visited the Maggid of Mezritch together with Rabbi Shmelke.

When Rabbi Shmelke was called to serve as rabbi of Nikolsburg, Rabbi Levi Yitzhak took his place as rabbi of the nearby town of Ritchvol. Unfortunately, the *Mitnagdim* in the city pursued him relentlessly, causing him great anguish, such that one year on

Hoshana Rabba he was forced to flee the city. He marched on foot, etrog and lulav in hand, to the Maggid of Kozhnitz.

In 1765, he became rabbi of Zhilokov in the Polish district of Siedlce. Here too the *Mitnagdim* embittered his life. In 1771, he was appointed rabbi in Pinsk, Byelorussia. Again, when Rabbi Levi Yitzhak was visiting his master in Mezritch, the *Mitnagdim* attacked his home and destroyed all his household possessions, and even replaced him with an alternate spiritual leader.

From then on, Rabbi Levi Yitzhak became a wanderer, from city to city, in poverty and hardship. As a result of the harassment of the *Mitnagdim*, Rabbi Levi Yitzhak suffered a nervous break-down. Fortunately, he quickly recovered. At the age of forty-five, he finally found tranquility when he was elected, with much honor, to serve as *Mara DeAtra* (chief rabbi) of Berdichev, a major Jewish center in the Ukraine.

The community in Berdichev was one of the largest in Czarist Russia, and an important center of the hasidic movement. Rabbi Levi Yitzhak served there as rabbi until the end of his days – almost a quarter of a century.

Rabbi Levi Yitzhak found peace in this stronghold of Hasidism. There he began to spread his powerful spiritual light far and wide, and his inspiring influence continued to grow. Under his tutelage, Berdichev became a fortress of Hasidism and a beacon to a multitude of Jewish followers who came to bask in the glow of Rabbi Levi Yitzhak and listen attentively to his prayers and melodies.

Rabbi Levi Yitzhak was an accomplished scholar, and thousands of students flocked to his beit midrash, where they studied Torah and Hasidism with him. On Shabbat days he would teach the congregation, and even on weekdays he would often go out to the marketplace, gather large assemblies of listeners, and encourage them to follow the path of Torah and piety.

His home was open to all those who suffered poverty and desolation. His heart was full of compassion, as reflected even in his family name, Derbaremdiker, which means "the compassionate one." Rabbi Levi Yitzhak was beloved by his people, and many beautiful legends became associated with him.

As a longtime student of the great Maggid of Mezritch, Rabbi Levi Yitzhak would assiduously record in his notebook many of the innovative interpretations of the Torah taught by his rebbe. He is known for his major contribution in collecting and disseminating his teacher's creative work.

In addition to spreading knowledge of Torah and Hasidism, Rabbi Levi Yitzhak was deeply involved on a regular basis with the needs of the community. He would journey through cities and towns to collect funds for redeeming captives, bridal dowries, and feeding the poor.

For over two decades, he occupied the rabbinical seat of Berdichev. On the twenty-fifth day of the month of Tishrei, 1809, he was called to the heavenly court.

Rabbi Nahman of Breslov called him, during his life, "the Glory of Israel." When Rabbi Levi Yitzhak died, Rabbi Nahman said, "Whoever has open eyes can see that the light of the universe has been extinguished, and the world has become dark." The Seer of Lublin eulogized, "Every day I set aside an hour to thank God for sending to the world an exalted, holy soul such as Rabbi Levi Yitzhak."

After Rabbi Levi Yitzhak's death, the town never crowned another rabbi to take his place, instead relying on *dayanim*, rabbinical arbiters, for guidance.

Many rabbis exhibited the virtues of Rabbi Levi Yitzhak, such as piety, love of Israel, advocacy for the Jewish people, and recognition of the uniqueness of the Jewish soul. However, it was only Rabbi Levi Yitzhak who rose to the high level of *melitz yosher*, a living example of a devoted and compassionate Jew who pleaded before the Master of the universe, compelling Him, as it were, to forgive and excuse the sins of the Israel. It was only Rabbi Levi Yitzhak who enumerated in full all the excellent qualities of the Jewish people, sang their praises, and chanted unceasingly the liturgical phrase, "Who is like Your people Israel?"

Furthermore, Rabbi Levi Yitzhak would notice the sinners of Israel, find their treasured qualities, and discover reasons to praise every fault and failure found in them. As Eliezer Steinman, one of the great writers on Hasidism, put it:

> Love of Israel was, for this righteous man, not an attribute acquired through the conquering of hatred, the acquiring of knowledge, a rational decision, or force of habit; rather, it was an inborn quality, an essence of goodwill, a burning bush of kindness. Even the words of advocacy with which he defended the People of Israel, and every Jew, were not in the realm of intellect or abstract reflection, but rather products of his soul, his secret dialogue with his Maker.

There is a great deal of hyperbole in hasidic storytelling, and more than a little overstatement when tzaddikim praise one another. There was frequent disagreement among the scholars about the various tzaddikim. But regarding Rabbi Levi Yitzhak, there was no disagreement; he was unanimously crowned as one who loved his people and advocated for them with the very essence of his soul.

Rabbi Shneur Zalman of Liadi said of him: "The Almighty is a tzaddik above, and Rabbi Levi Yitzhak is a tzaddik below." Rabbi Barukh of Mezhibush, grandson of the Baal Shem Tov, said of him that the Seraphim (fiery angels) in heaven are jealous of his love of God and of his piety toward God. Rabbi Menahem Mendel of Kotzk, who was extremely sparing with praise, stated that "Rabbi Levi Yitzhak opened the Sanctuary of Love in the heavens." And Rabbi Nahman of Breslov eulogized him with this lament: "We have lost our true master, the head of Israel." Though in truth, he was the heart of Israel.

When it came to wisdom of the heart, Rabbi Levi Yitzhak was second to none. In the words of Rabbi Menahem Mendel of Kotzk, Rabbi Levi Yitzhak showed the way of love and devotion. It might be more precise to say that he did not show the way – he himself was the way. He did not offer comfort, but was a comfort in his very being. In the darkness of Jewish life in exile, Rabbi Levi Yitzhak was a shining light. He was not a tzaddik who performed miracles; he himself was a miracle, a living testimony to the power of faith sustaining our nation.

Even though Rabbi Levi Yitzhak was a person of calm temperament and a lover of peace, he was not spared controversy and did not live a life of tranquility. Yet after his death, he became the people's cherished example of one who is loving and beloved; beloved by God, beloved by man, respected by the hasidic community, and honored by all, even those far from hasidic life.

More than this, he succeeded in raising the prestige of the Hasidism of his day, and with his melodies gladdened hearts throughout the Diaspora. He was graceful and benevolent, and yet in his lifetime he was not successful in all things. He was, according to all the evidence, sickly, feeble in every way, prone to weakness and accidents. In his desire to bless his lulav and etrog, he put his hand through the glass door of the cabinet in which they were lodged, cutting it quite badly. He so loved the burning lights of Ḥanukka that he once grabbed the burning wick, singeing his fingers. When he drew water with which to knead the dough for matza, he was so excited, he almost fell into the well. Rabbi Levi Yitzhak was never at peace, forever eager to fulfill the mitzvot. At the end of every festival he could not sleep, since his arm longed for his tefillin; he would sit at the window awaiting the light of dawn.

Rabbi Levi Yitzhak's soul knew no rest; and if there is no rest, how can there be joy? It is a great irony that this righteous man, who serves to this day as a source of joy and wellspring of encouragement to weary souls, led a life of such pain; he who was constantly bringing pleasure to his Creator and satisfaction to others knew so little of it himself. Rather, he was afflicted by a certain mental illness, which his biographers only hint; and for a whole year this great sage was in deep distress.

In suffering in silence, in being offended but never offending, Rabbi Levi Yitzhak carried much pain in his soul. His was not the lot of pleasantness. He poured out his soul in prayer, in cries, in excitement, in song, and in complaints to the Master of the universe. He pleaded in humility with all those who opposed him, and spoke to them with sweetness and kindness. Yet many requited his kindness with malice.

But there is no use in complaining about past events and directing accusations against those long gone. We learn from Rabbi Levi Yitzhak that advocacy is better than accusations. Nothing useful comes from old resentments. There are many who drank, and who still drink, from the cup of ingratitude. In fact, we are not the first to wonder about the lot of Rabbi Levi Yitzhak. Rabbi Elimelekh of Lizhensk was asked, "May our master teach us: Rabbi Levi Yitzhak, the lover of Israel, why did he have so many enemies?" He answered, "This is nothing new! It's the same old story. Avraham Avinu, may he rest in peace, also had many enemies who insulted him, and Nimrod and his cohorts cast him into a fiery oven. A fiery oven is the inheritance of passionate people."

Rabbi Levi Yitzhak eschewed spiritual arrogance, the high-handedness that often comes with authority. He threw his lot in with the masses, identifying heart and soul with his fellow Jews. His dearest wish was to resemble the simple Jew; to wear his clothes and eat his food, to bear his burdens, to seem in every way to be one of the simple folk. He immersed himself within the people, eradicating every real or imaginary barrier between the average Jew and the great rabbi, between the crowd and its spiritual leaders. For him, this was the true definition of Hasidism: Who is a Hasid? One who sees himself as part of the congregation and is brother and friend to everyman.

Rabbi Levi Yitzhak's philosophy was that all Jews are holy, that all are outstanding people, all righteous, pious, and all wise. And since he was always in a state of burning enthusiasm, he felt that all Jews had similar zeal. He may have cast off his rabbinic trappings, but he could not remove the fiery cloak of passion which he always wore. He thus enlarged the sense of wonder and awe, of honor and piety surrounding him.

It is well known: "Who are the kings? The rabbis." The great Torah scholars were mindful not to sully their kingly image, and took care that there was no stain on their clothes. They even permitted themselves a very small amount of pride and demanded honor for the Torah.

And then came along a rabbi, a giant in Torah and one of the great scholars in Halakha, whose demeanor was one of complete humility, who surrounded himself with simple Jews, bore their burden, carried their heavy loads in the marketplace, dragged bundles of wood on his back to kindle ovens, mixed with the masses, and never promoted his own reputation, preached to others, or admonished them. Quite the opposite, he searched for merit in every simple, ordinary person – even sinners – and served as advocate for all.

They gazed at him in amazement. They could not understand the nature of this Rabbi Levi Yitzhak. He was no normal rabbi; he was peculiar, and did not behave the way rabbis are expected to behave. Was he not a great rabbi, an exceptional scholar? Did he not demand honor for the Torah?

But Rabbi Levi Yitzhak was indeed a great scholar, and there is no doubt that his way of life and general demeanor met the highest standards of Torah. Every discussion, every motion of his was imbued with Torah values, as befitted descendants of the great sages of the Jewish people, whose every conversation was itself a complete philosophy.

He would pray for the prosperity of the House of Israel every minute, and demand of the Blessed Holy One that He be kind and munificent to His people Israel, and offer them abundance – especially material blessings – and that the world would be filled only with goodness. The goal of all his requests for the termination of the exile was that the People of Israel would return to the Land of Israel, which is the source of all goodness, since the Creator has great joy when Israel is filled with goodness and blessings.

Our image of Rabbi Levi Yitzhak is of one who is forever present on the *bima*, draped in his tallit and tefillin, presenting his arguments to the Blessed Holy One along with his pleas for the holy People of Israel. Rabbi Levi Yitzhak was forever toiling for the common person, laboring for the community and with the community.

Unfortunately, we do not find any written record of even a minor reference to the events that occurred in his life. From this point of view, Rabbi Levi Yitzhak was especially neglected, compared to his colleagues, who had many faithful and admiring students, eloquent writers, who took great pains to lavish on their accomplished masters multitudinous references in pamphlets and booklets, going to great lengths to praise their teachers' accomplishments.

Whatever we do know about the life of Rabbi Levi Yitzhak is in the realm of hearsay, passed down from one generation to the next, not without confusion – myth piled upon myth. Over the course of the years, therefore, after his death (even two or three generations after his passing), Rabbi Levi Yitzhak became a legend. He became a celebrated (if highly embellished) hero. Multitudes crowned him with garlands of folklore, fanciful stories, of which I have assembled, edited, and included in this book only a small percentage. About these the sages wrote, "The tales of the righteous are greater than the creation of heaven and earth" (Ketubot 5a). Not in vain did Rabbi Nahman of Breslov write, "Through the tales of the righteous, the light of the Messiah continues in this world and wards off much trouble and darkness from the world" (*Book of Middot*).

Many rebbes excelled in their love of Israel. Only Rabbi Levi Yitzhak was lifted to the loftiest heights by our people as a shining example of their advocate.

Generations of Jews forgot how some of their folk defamed Rabbi Levi Yitzhak, and remembered only the blessings he said about his people, the praise and honor he heaped upon the scattered flock of Israel. They expunged the insults that were thrust upon him while he walked the earth, and chose to recall, out of deep honor, only the outstanding accomplishments and inspiring melodies he left behind. Rabbi Levi Yitzhak's reputation did not advance in his life, but his image grew greatly as it was passed on to the following generations. Leading rabbis thought that the mention of the name of Rabbi Levi Yitzhak was a cure for illness, and we believe that the mention of his name has special merit for the health of the soul. Thus we say that Rabbi Levi Yitzhak is an eternal light for the soul.

Rabbi Levi Yitzhak did not have a large group of Hasidim, nor did he nurture many disciples. His personality and his nature were not those of a rabbi, but of a burning torch. A torch does not produce followers, nor can the chapters of its life be recorded. A torch is held high, passed from one generation to the next. It burns eternally. Such is Rabbi Levi Yitzhak, a torch passed down the hands of time, and each generation praises his deeds.

It is my prayer to our Heavenly Father that my humble offering, *Loving and Beloved*, will be accepted by a wide community of readers, and will confirm the ethical principles of love of humanity, of being loving and beloved, as the Baal Shem Tov taught, "If you want to be loved – love others." In this way, we will come closer to our Heavenly Creator, and perfect the world under the sovereignty of the Almighty.

May it be God's will!

Simcha Raz
10th of Tevet, 5768
(yahrzeit of my mother, my teacher, Hannah-Malkah
Rakover – née Mandelbaum – of blessed memory)

Between Man and God

A Sign from Heaven

A certain Jew came to Rabbi Levi Yitzhak of Berdichev with this request: "Would the honored rabbi assist in a *din Torah* that I have with the Master of the universe?"

Immediately, Rabbi Levi Yitzhak convened his beit din.

The Jew argued thus: "I am a pauper, I have no possessions, and am obligated by the Torah to marry off my grown daughter. Is it not right that the Blessed Holy One provide me with the provisions for the wedding?"

Rabbi Levi Yitzhak ruled, with the consent of the other judges, that the complainant was justified in his request. He even gave him this verdict in writing.

The Jew was overjoyed, and set out for home with the verdict in hand. Suddenly, a strong wind swept in and blew away the paper with the verdict. The Jew ran after the paper, which flew into the lap of a gentile duke who was sitting in his carriage at the crossroads.

The Jew pleaded with the duke to return the paper. The duke, however, was curious to know what was written on this document which the wind had blown straight to him. The Jew was embarrassed to tell the duke, so the duke called upon a Jewish translator, asking him to copy the verdict into Polish.

The duke was pleased with what he heard. Even more so, he saw the fact that the document had blown specifically into his lap as a sign from above that he was meant to be the good emissary who would help the Jew with the provisions for the wedding.

And so he did.

Who Is Liable?

Rabbi Levi Yitzhak of Berdichev listened carefully to a preacher who stood and rebuked the crowd of Jews for their sins.

After the speaker completed his sermon, Rabbi Levi Yitzhak said to him: "Why did you deliver only half of your sermon? Return to the *bima* and deliver the other half. You reproved the Jews because of their sins; now it is only fair that you reprove their Father in heaven, who oppresses them in exile, torments them harshly, and allows evil enemies to torture and abuse them."

"They're Watching!"

It happened once that Rabbi Levi Yitzhak of Berdichev was traveling in a wagon. Suddenly, the wagon driver noticed a pile of hay lying at the side of the road, and no one was around. The driver descended from the wagon, intending to steal the hay. Rabbi Levi Yitzhak cried out:

"They're watching, they're watching!"

The wagon driver looked all around, and asked in surprise, "Who?"

Rabbi Levi Yitzhak replied, "The Blessed Holy One!"

There Is a God in the World

It was reported to Rabbi Levi Yitzhak of Berdichev:

"The spirit of the *Haskala* is spreading in our region, and with it apostasy and irresponsible and immoral conduct."

Rabbi Levi Yitzhak gathered several of his followers, gave them travel expenses, and charged them to travel to all the surrounding Jewish communities and to announce in the marketplaces a rousing decree in his name:

"I, Levi Yitzhak of Berdichev, hereby proclaim to all listeners: there is a God in the world!"

Doing God's Work

It happened once that Rabbi Levi Yitzhak of Berdichev noticed a man walking in great haste. There was a sense of urgency about him.

The rabbi stopped him and asked, "What is your occupation Reb Yid?"

"I have no time to talk with your honor right now," answered the man.

Rabbi Levi Yitzhak persisted and asked, "Nevertheless, what is it you do?"

The man replied, "I humbly request from your honor not to delay me right now. I am dealing with some pressing business."

But Rabbi Levi Yitzhak refused to let him alone, and said, "Alright, alright, your business is stressing you. And your business is immense. But I am not asking you about your many businesses, but about your one main occupation. What is it?"

The man looked at him with surprise; he did not understand what the rabbi was talking about.

Rabbi Levi Yitzhak explained: "All your hard work is for the Blessed Holy One, in other words, to nourish the soul which God gave you. But your daily bread is the responsibility of the Holy Creator, while your job is to serve God. Therefore, why do you neglect your one job and run after the tasks of the Blessed Holy One?"

Don't Run

Rabbi Levi Yitzhak of Berdichev noticed a man running in the street, and asked him, "Reb Yid, what are you running after?"

"I'm running to make a living," he replied.

"Dear Reb Yid, who is to say your livelihood is in front of you, and you must chase after it? Perhaps it is behind you, and you are running away from it?"

His Paths Are Hidden

"There are worlds in which one can see the face of the *Shekhina* (Divine Presence).

These are the upper worlds, in which are revealed love and awe of God.

But in our world, His kingdom is hidden and His ways are concealed.

All the worlds – from the world in which the Throne of Glory is
      found, to the lower world – long to worship God, the liv-
      ing Creator,
Since all their vitality comes to them from Him.
Those who live in the lower world, the world of humans,
Desire that God enlighten their world,
Just as He always enlightens the upper worlds.
They desire that His ways and His kingdom be revealed to light
      the world,
And that all humans will worship Him.
Like misers who dream of wealth,
So do those who live in the world below dream and long
That His ways and His kingdom will be revealed,
Since they are poor in knowledge of God."

Between Man and His Fellow Man

The Sanctuary of Love

Rabbi Shmuel of Sokhatshov, author of *Shem MiShmuel*, told his followers:

My grandfather, Rabbi Menahem Mendel of Kotzk, was asked by one of his Hasidim: "May our master please teach us, why was there great love among Hasidim in the first generation, which has expired in our time?"

Rabbi Menahem Mendel answered: "There is a sanctuary in heaven above, called love. It was opened by Rabbi Levi Yitzhak of Berdichev, for love of friends, for devotion of Hasidim. What did the evil people of the generation do? They used the light of that love for strange and foreign passions.

"The righteous people of that generation gathered together – and sealed the door of that sanctuary. Hence, through our sins, the love among the Hasidim has ceased."

❧ ❧ ❧

Loving and Beloved

The Halakhic Decision

A *din Torah* between two business agents took place in the court of Rabbi Levi Yitzhak in Berdichev. The stronger did not agree to pay the other his share, in accordance with the decision of the court.

Immediately, Rabbi Levi Yitzhak sent a messenger of the beit din to summon the stronger agent. When he appeared, Rabbi Levi Yitzhak said to him:

"You should know that I also have expertise in the world of brokerage. I am the agent between the Jewish people and their Father in Heaven. I present the merits of Israel in the heavens, and bring back for them an abundance of blessings. Once, I made an exchange like this with the Master of the universe. I noticed that the Jewish people had three kinds of merchandise: sins, transgressions, and crimes. And up in heaven I also saw three kinds of merchandise: forgiveness, pardon, and atonement. I offered an exchange in heaven, and they agreed immediately. But they advised me to first speak to the people.

"I spoke with them, and at first they did not agree to the exchange. I negotiated with them and said to them, 'If you are not satisfied with these three wares that I brought down to you from heaven, then I will add three more: my son, my life, and my sustenance.' I ascended to heaven and requested these additions, and they agreed. Then I was asked in heaven, 'What do you want as payment for your mediation?' I answered that I do not want anything. But I trust that the Blessed Holy One will reward me in some fashion.

"The Holy One said to me, 'Levi Yitzhak, this is your reward: the additional goods that you listed, your son, your life, and your sustenance, are yours to distribute to whom you wish, and to take from whom you wish.'

"And know now," concluded Rabbi Levi Yitzhak, "that if you fulfill the terms of the legal decision, and immediately pay your debt, well and good. If not, Levi Yitzhak will punish you, as is your due, according to the strict letter of the law."

The stubborn businessman stood his ground, and ridiculed Rabbi Levi Yitzhak. He went home and mocked the words of the rabbi in front of his wife. Even as he spoke, he fell ill with malaria and began to scream: "My head, my head, oy! My whole body is shivering!" Doctors rushed to his side, but nothing helped.

When the man saw that he was on the threshold of death, he repented and sent his wife with the bundle of money required to pay off his debt, according to the ruling of Rabbi Levi Yitzhak.

A Sharp Tongue

Rabbi Levi Yitzhak did not waver when it came to financial disputes. He upheld not only his authority, but also his honor, and didn't spare those who behaved irreverently his sharp tongue.

It happened once that one of the disputants in a financial case, who was looking for an excuse to evade the judgement of Rabbi Levi Yitzhak, asked, "Since when is the rabbi of Berdichev an expert in matters of commerce?"

Rabbi Levi Yitzhak responded immediately with a mild jab:

"I tend to agree that with regard to heavenly matters your honor is more of an expert than I. In matters of Torah study, your honor is more adept than I. In areas of piety, your honor excels. But in matters of the world of commerce, I am an authority. In such matters, I am quite at home. Thus, your honor is obliged to accept my decision."

At the Meal of the Seven Shepherds

Often an honest but ignorant person would join Rabbi Levi Yitzhak at his table, and the group of students would look at him unkindly, since he was not at all able to grasp the meaning of the words of the tzaddik. After all, what was a boor doing among scholars? However, the naive gentleman did not take offense.

Finally, the students approached the rabbi's wife and requested that she send the fool on his way. But she was unwilling to do so without the permission of the tzaddik. So she related to her husband the doubts and request of the students.

The rabbi replied: "In the future, when the seven shepherds are seated at a holy feast – Adam, Seth, Methuselah on the right side; and Abraham, Jacob, Moses on the left, and David in the middle; and an empty-headed ignoramus arrives to join them – whose name is Levi Yitzhak – it seems to me that they will nod their heads to the fool, and greet him kindly."

Love of the Jewish People

"Since one God created all of us,
And the souls of Israel come from a single source,
When one of us feels pain,
His friend should feel it too.
And when one Jew experiences joy,
His friend should feel it too,
Like a person who feels pain in one limb,
And the whole body senses it."

Removing the Hatred in My Heart

"Until I expunge the flaw of hatred from my heart,
I cannot view myself as a man,
And I imagine myself as though I am not truly alive."

The Coming of the Messiah

I Await Him Every Day

His whole life, Rabbi Levi Yitzhak of Berdichev awaited the coming of the Messiah.

It happened that *tena'im* (terms of an engagement) were written for Rabbi Levi Yitzhak's granddaughter. Rabbi Levi Yitzhak examined the document.

He read it, and tore it up; then he shouted, "You don't believe in the coming of the Messiah! You wrote that during this year you will still be living in exile."

Rabbi Levi Yitzhak ordered that the following be added to the document: "The wedding will take place, *im yirtze Hashem*, with good fortune, in Jerusalem, the Holy City. If, God forbid, the righteous Messiah does not come this year, the wedding will be held in Berdichev."

Speedily, in Our Time

Rabbi Levi Yitzhak of Berdichev had a servant named Moshe, a simple, coarse man, who loved to eat and sleep. Once Rabbi Levi

Yitzhak asked him, "Moshe, what will you do when the Messiah comes?"

He answered, "I will eat abundantly, and I will get myself an ample supply of spirits, and I'll drift into a deep sleep."

"Moshe, what are you saying? Will you not go to greet the Messiah?"

"If the Messiah wants to come, he can come even without my welcoming him."

"And what will you do, Moshe, if the Messiah takes us out of the exile, and brings us to *Eretz Yisrael*? Will you come along with us?"

"How do I know? If I happen to wish to have a rest, surely I will stretch out on my bed and go to sleep."

Rabbi Levi Yitzhak broke out crying, and said, "Alas, pity on the Messiah, since Moshe will not be there to greet him. And pity also on Moshe, who does not understand that our great Messiah is the righteous redeemer, and will not go to greet him with song and dance."

Rabbi Levi Yitzhak cried and cried, until Moshe felt pity for his rabbi and said, "Rabbi, I am a simple man. God forbid that I should lie to my rabbi. What do I, Moshe, understand about the Messiah? I know about fish and meat and wine. Sweet sleep, as well, I know is a pleasure. But what do I understand about the Messiah? Now that I see my rabbi crying over the Messiah, I too believe that the Messiah is a wonderful thing."

As Moshe spoke, he too began to cry.

Rabbi Levi Yitzhak began to dance with joy, and cried out, "Come see, Master of the universe! Even Moshe wants the Messiah to come. And only You...only You, O God, are delaying the redemption, may it come speedily, in our time."

When Will the Messiah Arrive?

Once, when Rabbi Levi Yitzhak was seated at the table with his students, he said to them: "Let's try to understand the difficult passage in the Talmud in which the Messiah is asked when he will come, and he answers with a verse from the Book of Psalms, 'Today, if you would but heed God's charge...' (95:7). What makes this passage difficult is this: How can the Messiah say he will come today if we heed God's voice, when he sees that Elijah the prophet did not come yesterday? As it is written in scripture, 'Lo, I will send the prophet Elijah to you before the coming of the awesome, fearful day of the Lord' (Mal. 3:23).

"And do you know, my brothers," continued the rabbi, "why it is really important that Elijah the prophet precede the Messiah? Because people are steeped in the emptiness of this world, and are constantly busy with vanity. One person is excited about the new house he wants to buy, another about the yield of his crops, a third is worried that he might not get a good price for his harvest. In order for the Messiah to come to such people, Elijah the prophet must precede him by at least one day, to announce his coming, so that we can shake off our foolish habits and prepare ourselves to greet him.

"But if a day comes, a day in which we truly listen to God's voice – namely, a day in which we completely throw away the emptiness of this world and wait with all our heart for the coming of the redeemer – then there will be no need for the coming of Elijah the prophet."

Little by Little

A certain non-believer mentioned to Rabbi Levi Yitzhak of Berdichev that even the greatest scholars failed in their faith by believing in false messiahs, and in so doing misled the public. For example,

Rabbi Akiva thought that the rebel Bar Kokhba was the Messiah, and because of this treated him with honor and awe.

The rabbi replied with a parable: "It happened once that the only son of the king was stricken with a serious illness. Several physicians were gathered to consult together. One doctor suggested placing a piece of cloth dipped in pungent ointment on the patient's wounds. Another doctor objected that the young, spoiled prince would not be able to tolerate the harsh pain that such a strong ointment would cause. A third doctor suggested drugging the prince to anesthetize him so he would not feel the pain that the ointment would cause. A fourth doctor claimed that the anesthetizing drug might injure the prince's heart, since his organs were weakened by the disease. A fifth doctor suggested giving the prince the drug a little at a time, in teaspoonfuls, every few hours so that he would wake now and then, and his heart would not be harmed from the drug. And that is what they did."

Rabbi Levi Yitzhak continued: "The soul of Israel has been ill, and so the Blessed One gave it the strong ointment of exile to heal its wounds, and gave it an anesthetizing drug of foolishness to withstand the pains of the exile. But in order not to destroy the soul entirely by the darkness of the exile, He awakens it from time to time with small spoonfuls of deceptive hope, with false messiahs, and then puts it to sleep again. This will continue until the night of exile passes, and the true Messiah appears. And this is why, sometimes, even the eyes of the wise are blinded. But because they assist false messiahs, they are actually like healers."

The Time Has Come

It happened once that during the *Ne'ila* service on Yom Kippur, Rabbi Levi Yitzhak of Berdichev felt a surge of strength in his prayers, and with intense alertness stood at the *amud*, and stopped praying. The congregation stood quietly with great excitement. Suddenly, he roused himself from his deep concentration, and quickly concluded the prayers.

At the end of the day, the rabbi explained that he had made a supreme effort in his prayers to bring the Messiah, since they can no longer wait and the time has come; and he had almost succeeded. But suddenly he sensed that a certain Jew in the synagogue felt very weak from the fast, and if he tarried even a little the man might die. So he immediately completed his prayers, and the opportunity was lost.

In the World to Come
"A person's strength is drawn after his thoughts.
A person who thinks thoughts of holiness, and mourns over
　　　Jerusalem,
Is purified and gains a measure of the joy of Jerusalem,
As it will be in the World to Come."

Faith and Trust

This I Learned

Once, when Rabbi Levi Yitzhak of Berdichev returned from his travels, his father-in-law said to him, "I am prepared to forgive you for being drawn in by the Hasidim, provided you tell me what you learned from the Maggid of Mezritch."

Rabbi Levi Yitzhak replied that he had learned from the Maggid that God in heaven is the Creator of the world.

"Who doesn't know that?" his father-in-law scoffed, and summoned the maidservant.

"Do you know who created the world?" he asked her.

She answered: "God in heaven."

"Everyone can say that," explained Rabbi Levi Yitzhak, "but only one who learned it from the mouth of the great Maggid of Mezritch can *know* it."

Healing Through Faith

Rabbi Levi Yitzhak was once stricken by a very serious illness, and the doctors despaired of his recovery. He appeared to be at death's door. His eyes were shut, and all were certain that his soul had departed. Lights were kindled at the head of his bed, and those close to him sat in the outer room.

Suddenly, a thump was heard from the inner room. His friends rushed in and found Rabbi Levi Yitzhak lying on the floor. They lifted him onto the bed. They felt his pulse and saw that he was alive. They extinguished the candles which were at the head of his bed. He opened his eyes and mumbled a few words. It was clear that he had come back to life.

The next day, his friends came, and again they found him near death in his room. They again lit candles at the head of his bed, and sat in the next room praying for his soul. Again, they heard a thump from the inner room. They entered and found him lying on the floor. They lifted him onto the bed and saw that he was still alive.

When his friends returned on the third day, they entered his room and found their teacher sitting at the table studying Talmud. It appeared that he had completely recovered. They could not believe their eyes. When Rabbi Levi Yitzhak noticed their surprise, he said to them, "Here is a true story. Three days ago, my illness was very serious, and I became extremely weak. I could not move a limb. But my mind was completely well, thank God.

"I said to myself, 'Levi Yitzhak, you believe in the Blessed Creator, who is all-powerful. Can He not immediately bring you a complete recovery?' Then a different thought came to me and proved me wrong: 'No, Levi Yitzhak, you do not believe with perfect faith. You would like to believe, but truthfully, you don't.' Then a third thought came to me, contradicting the second: 'I truly believe with a full heart that the Blessed God can heal me immediately. And I'll prove it. I will immediately overcome, get out of bed, go to the table, and study a book.' And so I did.

"When, on the first day, I – apparently – did not truly believe with a full heart, I stumbled and fell. The second time I also did not have full faith, and I fell again. But today I overcame, and arose with full and complete faith that the Blessed One can heal me in the blink of an eye. And so it was. The Blessed One helped me since I believed truly and completely."

Perhaps

An educated man, one of the *maskilim*, heard about the tzaddik of Berdichev and traveled there to argue with him, as was his wont, and to undermine the rabbi's arguments and proofs about the truth of his beliefs.

When he entered the tzaddik's room, the traveler noticed that he was pacing back and forth, lost in thought, a book in his hand, entirely unaware of the guest who had entered. Finally, the tzaddik paused, glanced at him casually, and said, "Perhaps it's true."

The man lost his nerve. So awesome was the sight of the tzaddik, so solemn the sound of his words, that he went weak at the knees.

Finally, the rabbi turned toward him and spoke to him gently: "My son, the giants of Torah, with whom you have argued, wasted their words on you, and you, when you left them, laughed at them. They could not show you God, nor prove to you His sovereignty. Neither can I do that. But, my son, think deeply, because perhaps it is true."

The wise man mustered his inner strength to respond, but that awe-inspiring word "perhaps," which echoed in his ears over and over, ended his resistance.

Lottery

A certain Hasid came to Rabbi Levi Yitzhak of Berdichev and poured out his heart. His situation was dire; he had gotten himself into great debt and no one knew about it, since until now he had been a very wealthy man. But he had recently lost his money in unfortunate business ventures.

The rabbi suggested to him, "Buy yourself a lottery ticket, and, God willing, this will save you."

The Hasid replied, "I do not doubt, heaven forbid, that the promise of the rabbi will come true. But who knows when, since it sometimes takes years to win a lottery. Meanwhile, my creditors will start to torment me, and, in addition, I have a daughter who has come of age and I must marry her off."

Rabbi Levi Yitzhak promised that the Blessed One would provide funds for him soon, even before he would win the lottery. The Hasid, of course, carried out the suggestion of the tzaddik and bought a lottery ticket.

On his way home, the Hasid came upon a hotel and decided to spend the night there. That same night, an important dignitary who was traveling in the area also retired to the hotel and dreamt that in the hotel there was a certain Jew who had a lucky lottery ticket, and that he must endeavor to switch tickets with him, since the Jew's ticket would surely win, and his was worthless. The dignitary awakened, then fell asleep again, and dreamt the same dream a second time.

He got out of bed and ordered his servant to investigate and see if there was an itinerant Jew in the hotel. The servant found the Hasid and brought him to the dignitary, who asked if he had a lottery ticket. The Hasid said yes, and the dignitary responded, "I also have a lottery ticket. Let us exchange tickets, and I'll add several gold pieces to what you paid."

The Hasid refused, and told the dignitary that even if he gave him many gold pieces he would not exchange tickets.

The dignitary offered him up to a thousand gold pieces if he would only exchange tickets, but the Hasid stood his ground and refused. The dignitary then became angry and ordered his servant to take the ticket from the Hasid by force. The servant attacked the Hasid and took the ticket from him. The dignitary said to the Hasid, "Nevertheless I do not want to steal from you, so here are the thousand gold pieces that I offered you and my lottery ticket as well."

Against his will, the Hasid accepted the money and ticket and thought to himself, "This too is for the best." He went home and made a lavish wedding for his daughter.

A short time later, the ticket which the dignitary had made the Hasid take was the winning lottery ticket for a large amount of money. The Hasid traveled to Berdichev to see the rabbi. The tzaddik said to him:

"I saw that your fortune had completely turned, and I was forced to send the Master of Dreams to influence the dignitary, so that he would exchange lottery tickets with you. I knew that his ticket would win. The thousand gold pieces that he added were because you told me that you had to marry off your daughter immediately. Thus, even from the outset you had a small salvation, and afterward came the major salvation."

The Hasid returned to his home, wealthier than he had ever been.

The Jewish People

Act For Your Glory!

"Do, if not for our merit, at least for the honor of the tefillin,
Which are called in the Talmud 'glory'…
A plain and simple Jew, if it happens, heaven forbid,
That his tefillin fall on the ground by mistake,
He would rush to pick them up and kiss them, and be troubled
    and distressed,
And would fast several fasts…
And You, Master of the universe,
For eighteen hundred years, Your tefillin,
On which it is written, 'Who is like Your people Israel, a unique
    nation on earth' (Berakhot 6a),
Have become mockery and scorn, dragged through mud and trash,
In places that are impure and defiled,
So how can You tolerate this, Master of the universe, for so long?
And how can You do this, in accordance with the Law?"

No Complaints

Once, in the dead of night, Rabbi Levi Yitzhak awakened his servant and said to him, "Take a flask of brandy together with a small cup and come with me."

He went with him to the hostel for the needy in Berdichev, a place the poor, indigent vagabonds frequented. He awakened one of the men from his sleep, poured him a cup of brandy, and said to him, "Would you like to drink a bit of brandy? Here's a cup. Take it and drink."

The man opened his eyes. He saw a distinguished-looking Jew standing before him holding a cup of brandy in his hand, and had no idea that this man was the local rabbi. In great surprise, he said, "But dear sir, how can I drink before performing the ritual of handwashing?"

Rabbi Levi Yitzhak tried to awaken another man, then a third, but all of them gave the same answer: "We cannot taste even a drop without the ritual washing of hands."

He left them and went, together with his servant, to the bathhouse, where the *Shabbos goy* slept. Rabbi Levi Yitzhak awakened him, handed him the bottle of brandy, and this fellow guzzled it down in one gulp.

From there Rabbi Levi Yitzhak went to his beit midrash, opened the doors of the holy ark, and called out: "Master of the universe! See what a difference there is between the Jewish people and the gentiles…. And You, as it were, still have grievances and complaints about the nation You have chosen."

No Comparisons

"The ideal is not to be loved merely because Esau is hated.

"We must aspire to be worthy, on our own merit, of the love of the Creator, without the need to compare ourselves to others who are less worthy than we.

"This is the meaning of the prayer (recited after Psalms), 'May Your people not be dependent on one another, and not on another nation': that Israel be excellent and exalted on their own merit, to the point that there will be no need to compare any Jew to another Jew less worthy, or to compare the Jewish people to another people, in order to prove that the other is far less worthy."

The Glory of Israel

When a Jew would denigrate a fellow Jew, Rabbi Levi Yitzhak of Berdichev would approach him and whisper in his ear, "My dear son, you are speaking ill, not of your neighbor; rather you are slandering the Blessed Holy One. In God's tefillin it is written: 'Who can be compared to Your people Israel?' Surely you did not mean to say what you said about Him."

Keep Your Word

As was his custom, Rabbi Levi Yitzhak would argue with the Blessed Holy One: "Master of the universe! You became betrothed to us because we are beloved to You, as written in the liturgy, 'You loved us and desired us,' and 'You will be My treasured people.'

"You represented Yourself to us as wealthy, as it is written (Hag. 2:8): 'Mine is the silver and Mine is the gold, says the Lord.'

"Therefore, we established a financial relationship. Thus I ask of You, keep Your word and discharge the debt, as You promised at the time of the engagement, since in our special situation we need a large dowry."

Jewish Unity

"Master of the universe,
There are six hundred thousand letters in the Torah,
The Jewish people are comprised of six hundred thousand souls.
Take heed, Master of the universe, when the Torah is whole,
It is forbidden to erase even one letter.
But when it is divided into five books,
It is not forbidden to erase anything.
The same is true of the Jewish people.
When there is total unity,
No man can be destroyed."

Joy and Sadness

The Heart of Worship

"There is great joy in all worlds,
When a Jew has bread to eat and clothing to wear,
Because he can then easily fulfill
'Serve the Lord with joy' (Ps. 100:2),
Which is the heart of divine worship."

Joy

"Sometimes, all of a sudden, joy permeates one's being,
And its source is not known.
What is the cause of this joy?
The truth is
That at that very moment, his name is mentioned for good
In the heavenly spheres."

The Ever-Renewing Spring

"There are two kinds of sorrow, and two kinds of joy.

"Two kinds of sorrow, wherefore?

"There is the sorrow of a man in distress, who frets over a lost article or a different mishap that happened to him, and he is bowed, gloomy, and depressed.

"About such a one our sages taught: 'The Divine Presence does not dwell where there is sadness, only where there is the joy of a mitzva' (Shabbat 30b).

"But another kind of sadness is when one sorrows about the fleeting days of his life, and he examines his deeds, and perseveres in perfecting his soul.

"This kind of sorrow is a source of blessing and strength to rouse him to improve his way of life.

"So it is with joy:

"There is joy that is banal and insipid, which is the joy of a fool, who does not feel any lack in himself and is not at all concerned to improve himself.

"But one who is steeped in the joy of goodness and knowledge resembles one whose house has burned down, and not only is he not melancholy, but he hopes that God will fill his need; and when, through the strength of his hope and his faith, he becomes confident and begins to rebuild his home, for every stone that he brings and affixes his heart is like an ever-renewing spring of joy."

Enthusiasm

"Enthusiasm serves as a test
To discern whether the Blessed One has
Pleasure from the person's worship,

And when this person sees that his heart burns
And becomes more and more passionate,
It is a sign that the Blessed One has pleasure from his worship,
And thus Heaven assists him in his prayers.
Another great attribute of enthusiasm is that
Through its agency, whoever does a mitzva has gained more than
     the doing of this one mitzva.
For example, one who lays tefillin has accomplished just the
     mitzva of tefillin.
But one who yearns to perform this mitzva in order to bring sat-
     isfaction to his Creator,
His yearning includes all the mitzvot, and he is considered as
     though he has performed all the mitzvot.
And know that enthusiasm is expressed only through joy,
Because joy is rooted in fire. And though most of the joy is in
     the heart,
The joy of the heart can cease from time to time.
But when one expresses his joy in words,
The joy grows and grows, and there is no limit to the enthusiasm."

Loving-Kindness

Eulogizing the Deceased

Rabbi Shlomo Yosef Zevin (d. 1978) told the following story:

When Rabbi Levi Yitzhak was chief rabbi in Berdichev, a well-to-do Jewish gentleman, who was known as a miser, passed away. The *ḥevra kaddisha* demanded from his heirs a huge sum for the burial plot, but they did not agree to pay it. It was decided to take the matter to Rabbi Levi Yitzhak.

When they approached the tzaddik and told him about the matter, he became very upset by the news of the man's death, and ordered that the inheritors pay only what they desire, out of their own good will. He also requested that they inform him about the time of the funeral, since he himself wished to take part in the mitzva of the burial.

The *ḥevra kaddisha* were astonished at hearing this, but nevertheless fulfilled the demand of the tzaddik to the letter. When word went out to the community that the tzaddik himself would be participating in the funeral, the entire community came, paying great respect to the deceased.

When the members of the community returned from the funeral, they asked the tzaddik, "What moved you to extend such honor to a miser like him?"

The tzaddik replied, "This man appeared before me in three different *dinei Torah*, and in all three he won his case. Therefore he is worthy to be shown such honor.

"The first *din Torah* was this: It happened that a certain wine merchant was accustomed to receive money from store-keepers of his town to buy wine for them from the big city. On one occasion, after he had purchased the wine and wanted to pay for it, behold, the money was gone. He had carried a very large sum of money in his pocket, and it was lost. The man let out a huge cry from his heart, and then fainted. People tried to arouse him, without success. At last he awakened, but the moment he saw that the money had not been found, he fainted once more. Doctors were rushed to the scene, and proclaimed that unless the money was found the merchant would not recover.

"As it happened, the deceased gentleman, whom we buried today, was visiting the city. When he saw the commotion sur-rounding the man who had fainted, he announced that he had found the lost money. The merchant awakened when he heard the announcement, and the visiting gentleman immediately handed him the money. The merchant took the money, thanked the man, and went on his way.

"However, truth to tell, the man we buried today had not found the money at all. He simply saw that the merchant's life depended on this money, and decided to save him. So he said that he had found the money, while actually paying the dealer the large sum from his own pocket.

"Among those who surrounded the merchant who had fainted, and witnessed the whole event, was the person who actu-ally found the money. His selfish instinct prevented him from returning it. But when he saw the noble act of a stranger, who offered a large sum of money from his own pocket and told everyone that he was the finder, his conscience began to trouble him. From that point on, this feeling disturbed him more and more, until he regretted the whole affair, and could not rest until he decided to return the money to the man from Berdichev.

"He traveled to Berdichev, came to the man whom we buried today, and related to him that he was actually the one who found the money, that he knew it was he who had paid the merchant from his own pocket, and therefore he now wished to return the funds.

"But our deceased refused to accept the money. 'You have no business with me,' he said. 'I was fortunate enough to merit the mitzva that God presented to me, of saving a life, and I am not prepared to relinquish it.'

"After a while the two men decided to bring the dispute to a rabbinic tribunal. They came before me and presented their claims. The first one argued that he had found it and must pay, and the other argued that the finder should have paid the merchant at the time, and he himself is not required to take the money.

"The deceased was declared the winner in our tribunal. The verdict was that he did not have to accept the money against his will.

"The second *din Torah* was this: A poor man from Berdichev wanted to leave his home and try his luck in far-off places, but his wife did not permit him to do so. The man thought it over, came to his wife, and told her that a certain wealthy man had hired him as an official in his business. He would be sending him on business trips to various cities, and had promised that every Thursday the treasurer of his firm would pay his wife a fixed sum toward his wages. The wife agreed, and the husband set off on his travels.

"When Thursday arrived, the woman came to the treasurer to receive the wages, but the treasurer claimed that he did not know what she was talking about. He knew nothing at all about her husband. The woman began to scream that her husband is not a liar, God forbid, and he did not deceive her. The treasurer resented the woman's accusations. The wealthy man overheard the woman's cries, and walked in to ask what all the noise was about. They told him the matter. The wealthy man said, 'The woman is right! I myself hired her husband as an official, and promised to pay his wife the stated amount every week.'

"The man ordered the treasurer to pay her the correct amount every Thursday. And in the course of time, the Blessed Holy One brought success to the husband, and he became very wealthy.

"After a long while, the husband returned home. Following the excitement of the reunion, the woman related to him that, thanks to God, she did not suffer any lack, since the wealthy man regularly paid her the weekly stipend. The husband was amazed. He took a satchel of coins, calculated how much the wealthy man had dispensed for his 'wages,' and went to the rich man – our deceased – to try and repay him everything. But the man refused to accept it. 'You have no business with me,' he said. 'I have never met you. I only gave what I gave to your wife as a gift, and I do not have to accept anything from you.'

"Ultimately, they came before my rabbinic tribunal, and, once again, the claim of the wealthy man was accepted.

"This was the third *din Torah*: A certain gentleman who had become impoverished arrived in Berdichev, where, he had heard, there was a business in which he could earn some money. However, he required a certain sum to invest in this venture, and did not have a single zloty. Eventually he approached the same wealthy man, our deceased, and asked for a loan in that amount from the local Free Loan Society.

"The wealthy man asked, 'Is it not true that you, sir, are not a wealthy person, so what security can you give me for this loan?'

"The man replied, 'My security is the Master of Security (God).'

"Having heard this reply, the wealthy man immediately granted the loan, saying, 'I can certainly, without doubt, rely on the Master of Security,' and he gave him the full amount.

"The poor man succeeded in business and earned much money. After a while, he went to the wealthy man to return the loan. He refused to accept it. 'I have already received my payment in full,' he said. 'When did you receive it?' cried the man, in great surprise. 'I have not yet returned a single zloty to you.'

"The wealthy man replied: 'Did you not tell me in your own words that I should lend you the money with the security of the Master of Security? The Master of Security has already repaid the debt to me, with interest.'

"Ultimately, they went to a *din Torah* and the wealthy man won his case yet again.

"After these three rabbinic tribunals," concluded Rabbi Levi Yitzhak of Berdichev, "surely this deceased man is worthy of honor."

Only then did the members of the community realize that the deceased pretended to be a miser so that he could give in secret, without anyone knowing just how charitable he was.

Two Jews Vying for a Mitzva

It happened that a Jewish merchant, a pious and upright man, returned from the great fair in Leipzig and passed through the city of Berdichev. When he arrived in the city, he alighted from his wagon, planning to stop at an inn. On the way, his wad of money fell out of his pocket, and he had no idea that it was gone.

When he passed the market, he wanted to make a purchase, and suddenly realized that his money was gone. He panicked and began to search for his money in all the pockets of his garments. But in vain, he had no money. He left the storekeeper and his wares, and went about searching for his lost money. He retraced his steps, searched and hunted on every path and trail, quizzed every passerby, but no one could help him.

What did this poor fellow, whose pockets were empty and whose heart was broken, do? He stood at the crossroads and proclaimed his loss. He cried and begged people to have mercy on him, to return his money and fulfill the mitzva of returning a lost object (Deut. 22:1–3). And in order to encourage those who would not normally rush to perform a mitzva, he offered a generous reward to whoever fulfilled this mitzva, besides the future reward the person would receive from the Blessed Holy One.

But it was as if he was calling in a wilderness. The crowd heard his wailing cry, and continued on their way. The unfortunate man did not despair. He stood and proclaimed his plight in the middle of the town. He was embittered by his loss, and his voice was pitiable.

At the same time, a young yeshiva student came out of his house on the way to morning prayers. His face was clear, his eyes sparkling, his clothes spotless, and under his arm he carried a bag with his tallit and tefillin. He walked slowly, unhurriedly making his way, completely engrossed in the talmudic passage which he had, just minutes before, finished studying. When he reached the market, he heard a frightening cry which interrupted his thoughts. He looked up and saw in the distance a large crowd surrounding an honorable gentleman, who was standing and crying like a child.

The young man's compassion was aroused at this sight, and instead of continuing on to the beit midrash, he turned toward the crowd. He immediately heard the voice of the man, crying, "Compassionate people! Have pity on me, and fulfill the mitzva of returning a lost article, for there is no mitzva greater than this."

The young man looked at the Jew, his face darkened from sadness, and reflected a bit, as one who is about to do something beyond his ability. He approached the man and said, "If you have certain proof that it is yours, I will return to you the money you have lost." The merchant's face lit up when he heard these words, and he immediately began to enumerate the specific bills that had been in his pocket: "I had this many one-ruble bills, this many five-ruble bills, and this many ten-ruble bills. In addition, I had ten rubles in coins, plus approximately two rubles in silver and copper." And he detailed all the coins that had been in his pocket.

When the young man heard the detailed account of the money, he took out his notebook and recorded it all. He then added it all up and said, "The total sum is correct, and the denominations of the bills match. The only thing I cannot remember are the silver and copper coins. I'll have to check on that. Don't worry! All these people standing here with us know me and my family. Please wait here then until I return. And if all the details you gave, in the presence of the community, are correct, I will return the money to you."

When the young man concluded his words he left, with all in agreement, and after a short while he returned, face aglow, with the money, according to the details given by the man. He gave it all, every zloty, to its owner. The merchant received his money from the yeshiva student and thanked him profusely for his kindness and honesty. When he tried to give the young man a reward, as he had promised, the latter refused to accept it.

The members of the community, witnessing all of this, rejoiced together with the merchant. They had not enough words with which to praise the young man, or glorify his good deed. The merchant thanked the young man again for his kindness, and they parted with each going his own way – the merchant to his town, and the young man to the synagogue to pray and pour out his heart to his Creator.

Weeks passed, months flew by, an entire year elapsed, and again it was time for the great fair in Leipzig, which the merchant was accustomed to attend. All year, the merchant was preoccupied, and his business distracted him, so that he completely forgot about the events that had occurred the year before when he had passed through Berdichev.

However, when the time for the great fair arrived and he began preparing himself to travel to Leipzig, the whole matter arose in his mind, and he planned to pass through Berdichev after the fair once again and seek out the young man and thank him for his good deed of the year before.

As he planned, so he did. He came to Leipzig, worked during all the market days, arranged his affairs well, and when the market days concluded, returned home by way of Berdichev. When he arrived he was very tired from the trip and checked into a hotel, hoping to rest a bit before seeking out the young man, so he could pay his respects well rested and in good spirits. He sat down for a bit, changed his clothes, and busied himself with this and that until lunchtime arrived. He feasted, recited the Grace after Meals, then lay down on his bed and fell deeply asleep. When he awoke, he saw the sun beginning to set. He got up quickly, washed his hands, put on his coat, tightened his belt, took his walking stick in hand, and went to the beit midrash of Rabbi Levi Yitzhak to recite the afternoon and evening prayers. When he entered the beit midrash, he found a small group, among whom was the young yeshiva student.

He started to approach the young man, but another man came in from the outside and greeted him. The merchant returned the greeting, and after these formalities the stranger asked the merchant, "What city do you come from, sir?" The merchant replied, "From such-and-such city." When he heard the name of the city, the man's face lit up, and he cried out in joy, "It has been a whole year that I am seeking a man from that city, and I have not been able to find him. Blessed be God who sent you now to me."

The merchant said with curiosity, "Who is this man you are seeking? What is his name? If he is from my city, I certainly know him, and if you have some good news for him I will gladly pass it on." The stranger said, "His name is such-and-such, he is a merchant, and I have good news for him." The merchant replied, "That is my name, and I am a merchant." The stranger said, "I have one more question to ask, and depending on your answer I will know exactly if you are the man I am seeking." The merchant replied, "Ask, and I will answer."

The stranger said, "Tell me, briefly, if last year you lost a certain amount of money in our city, as you were returning from the great fair in Leipzig." The merchant was bewildered when he heard this, but immediately composed himself and answered politely, "Yes, that is what happened." The stranger became excited and said, "Surely this is an act of God, for I have found what I was looking for. If what you are saying is accurate, and I have no doubt that you are the man who lost his money, I must act according to the law. Be ready tomorrow morning, and the two of us will go to a rabbinic tribunal, where you can describe exactly what you lost as is required by Jewish law, and I will perform the mitzva of returning a lost object."

The merchant became even more perplexed, and could hardly believe his ears. He looked directly at the stranger with puzzled eyes and asked, "What are you talking about? I got back my money, on the same day that I lost it, from a certain young man, after I described to him all the details of what I had lost, in front of a large crowd. In fact, the young man is right here in the beit midrash. Let's ask him, so that he can clarify the whole matter for us properly."

Meanwhile, a large number of people came in to recite their prayers, and saw the two men arguing. The crowd came closer to hear what they were discussing, and the matter became public knowledge. Then the merchant explained the matter again – that he does not know the stranger, never heard of him, and will not accept money from him that he has already received from someone else. And if the stranger intends to give him a gift, he should know that during his entire life the merchant benefited only from his own hard work, and never from the gift of any person, and today would be no different. He would not accept a gift, even if it was in the form of a returned lost object.

When he concluded his remarks, the merchant left the stranger and the others who had gathered, and went over to the young man who was sitting near a lectern in the corner, studying intently. However, the stranger followed him and hollered, "It is not I who gave you a gift, but this young man. What do you want from me? For a whole year I guarded this money. I held onto it carefully until it could reach its owner. And now that God has brought me to its owner, shall I not fulfill this mitzva? I shall not relinquish the opportunity to perform this mitzva! It belongs to me, and no one else has a share in it."

The young man overheard the stranger's claim, and got involved in the matter, saying, "What are you shouting about? This merchant is right. Lost objects generally don't return to their rightful owners even once, especially lost money, which cannot be definitely identified, and you want to reward him and return his lost money twice? Did he not already receive it from me? He is an honest man, and will not agree to accept money that is not his."

Then the stranger jumped up, angry, and cried out, "Did you give him back that which contained the money? Here in my hand is the wallet, with the money, which I have kept until now." The merchant suddenly remembered that the young man had returned the money without a wallet, and his arguments came to a halt. After this exchange, when the men had calmed down, they agreed to go to a rabbinic tribunal the next day, and do whatever the rabbi would decide.

The next day, the three disputants approached Rabbi Levi Yitzhak, who greeted them in a friendly manner, saying, "Come into the office of the rabbinical tribunal, where the judges sit to adjudicate, and present your claims before them."

They replied, "It is our intent to present our cases only before the honored rabbi. If the hour is inconvenient for you, we can come at another time, provided that your honor is the judge." The rabbi attempted to put them off with various excuses, but when he saw that they were determined, he brought them into a special room, where he sat at the head of the table, and invited them to present their claims.

The merchant began and told his side of the matter: "Last year, this yeshiva student returned to me a sum of money that I had lost. Two days ago, I came back to Berdichev and met this gentleman, who told me that he found my money, and has been searching for me for a year, in his desire to fulfill the mitzva of returning lost objects. When I heard what he said, I was astounded and told him that my money had already been returned to me, and that I had no intention of accepting the money twice. And that if he desired, he could come with me to the young man, since he was actually the one with whom he had an argument, and they could settle the matter between them."

When the Jew heard the merchant's words, he could not restrain himself. He jumped up as if a snake had bitten him and, shouting, interrupted him: "I am not interested in what happened between you and the young man. I have no argument with him, since he is not the one who lost the money – you are. I am the one who found the wallet with the money, and I guarded it the whole year until I could find its owner. Even you admit that the young man returned the money to you without the wallet, proving that he did not find the money. This is evidence that the entire mitzva belongs to me, and no one else has a share in it. I will not yield. The mitzva is entirely mine."

When the man finished, the yeshiva student began his case: "It is true that I have no argument with this Jew. I know only one thing, which is that I was the first to return the money to the person who lost it. God is my witness. Everything I did was only so that the matter would not become public. Now that it has, against my will, I am not ready to relinquish the right to this mitzva, which is entirely mine. Even if the man gives me his entire fortune, I will not accept it from him."

Rabbi Levi Yitzhak sat quietly while the disputants argued their cases, and carefully noted every word they said. After they finished their presentations, silence reigned. No one said a word. The rabbi sat with his eyes shut and his face glowing. After a while, he opened his eyes and turned toward heaven, and said:

"Master of the universe! Who is like Your people Israel, a holy nation? Observe their holiness. Satan and the nations of the world claim that Jews are money grubbers. Let Satan and his entire contingent roam the earth to seek and find three greedy people like these, standing before God, who are not the sons of Abraham, Isaac, and Jacob. I am ready to grant them all of my portion in the World to Come, if they can find three gentiles who are as greedy as they.

"Dear God, give ear and heed their words: are such arguments found among the children of Esau and Ishmael? Two Jews claim ownership of one mitzva. Neither one is willing to concede to his fellow even one whit. I doubt there is a single judge among the judges of the nations before whom a matter like this has come.

"And now what am I to do? The disputants demand a rabbinical decision. I think that they are both right, but I cannot split this mitzva in half. In my humble opinion, I have no choice but to make a decision at Your expense, Creator of the universe. Are You not the Giver of mitzvot? From Your mouth, Israel was commanded to perform them, and You can see that they are fulfilling them with all their heart and soul. It is clear to me that You will agree with me."

After this, Rabbi Levi Yitzhak arose and said: "In the opinion of the earthly court and of the court on high, I am ready to pronounce my decision. Both disputants deserve full credit for this mitzva, and they both deserve the reward. The Blessed Holy One will forgo one mitzva, and the money will be distributed among the poor."

Great awe fell upon the disputants when they heard the decision of the holy rabbi, and they accepted it. That same day, the charity officers, led by the rabbi, distributed the recovered money to the poor folks of Berdichev in the presence of the three disputants. And the poor of Berdichev rejoiced and were glad.

≥ ≥ ≥

Hospitality

Rabbi Levi Yitzhak of Berdichev was visiting the city of Lvov, Poland. He came into the house of a certain wealthy, respected gentleman.

"Is it possible for me to rest overnight in your home?" asked Rabbi Levi Yitzhak, without revealing who he was.

"I have no room for passersby. Go and find an inn."

"A very small corner in one of your rooms will be quite sufficient. I won't be a bother to anyone."

"I have no room. If you can't find an inn, go to the *melamed* (local teacher), on the next street. He often accepts guests."

Rabbi Levi Yitzhak went to the home of the *melamed*, and was welcomed warmly.

When the rabbi walked down the road, a passerby recognized him. Immediately word got out that the holy rabbi of Berdichev had come to the city. It did not take long before a mob of people arrived and tried to squeeze into the house of the *melamed* to welcome the rabbi. Among them was the very same wealthy, respected man.

When the man came before Rabbi Levi Yitzhak, he said, "I ask forgiveness from our distinguished teacher and rabbi. I humbly request that you honor me with your presence as my visitor. All the righteous men who have come to the city have stayed in my house."

Rabbi Levi Yitzhak turned to the large crowd of people gathered before him and said: "Our father Abraham was well known for his gracious hospitality. When the angels came to him, the Torah relates that 'he took curds and milk and the calf that had been prepared and set these before them' (Gen. 18:8). What is the novelty here? Did not Lot do the same, as it says in the Torah, 'They turned his way and entered his house. He prepared a feast for them and baked unleavened bread, and they ate' (Gen. 19:3)? But we do not find anywhere that Lot was praised for being a hospitable person.

"Here is the difference: In the case of Lot it is written, 'The two angels arrived in Sodom....' (Gen. 19:1). In the case of Abraham, it is written, 'Looking up, he saw three men standing near him' (Gen. 18:2). Lot saw angels and invited them into his house, but Abraham saw simple men, travelers covered with dust, tired and thirsty, and entreated them, 'Please do not pass by your servant' (Gen. 18:3)."

⁂

Your Kindnesses Are Prayers

A poor wagon driver came to Rabbi Levi Yitzhak of Berdichev with a question. He was careful to recite the morning and evening prayers regularly, but he prayed alone, since he was unable to recite these prayers with a *minyan* in a synagogue because of his work hours. From early morning until sunset he would travel with his horse and wagon from village to village, and therefore could not join a *minyan* in the mornings and evenings, as required.

So he was asking the rabbi if he should quit his job and find different work, in order to be able to pray in a *minyan* on a regular basis.

Rabbi Levi Yitzhak replied with a question: "Tell me, please, when you meet someone on the road who is walking in the direction that you are traveling, do you take him in your wagon without payment?"

"Certainly," answered the wagon driver. "Can a Jew do otherwise?"

"If so," concluded Rabbi Levi Yitzhak, "you do not have to change jobs, since what you do is precious in the eyes of the Blessed Holy One – as much as praying in a *minyan*."

Giving in Secret

When Rabbi Yosef son of Reb Tzvi, author of *Toledot Yosef*, came to Berdichev to sell his books, he brought with him two hundred books and rent for a store. He put a display of open books in the window, so that passersby could review their content. But when those who came into the store heard the price, they shrugged their shoulders and went on their way.

When Rabbi Levi Yitzhak of Berdichev heard about this, he gave a sum of money to one of his young students to buy one hundred copies, and ordered him to pretend to bargain with Rabbi Yosef, in a way that Rabbi Yosef would not perceive the ruse. The young man went and bought one hundred books.

The next day, Rabbi Yosef came to Rabbi Levi Yitzhak and told him, with joy and wonder, that, thank God, one buyer purchased a hundred copies in one day!

Mitzva

A Father's Pride

"It states in the Zohar:
Every time a person performs a mitzva,
The Blessed Holy One takes pride and says:
'Such are the deeds of My children!'
And God recites praise about this person,
As a father who speaks and repeats
The words of his young child, who is beloved to him."

By My Life!

It happened once on Rosh HaShana that Rabbi Levi Yitzhak was standing in prayer, just before the shofar blasts, and he turned his eyes to heaven and said:

"Master of the universe! What complaints do You have against the People of Israel? By my very life, were it not that I have witnessed with my own eyes how the Jewish people fulfill Your mitzvot, give *tzedaka*, and perform good deeds, I would not at all believe that they had the strength to perform even one mitzva in this bitter exile."

≫ ≫ ≫

Seudat Mitzva

When Rabbi Levi Yitzhak was first appointed as head of the rabbinic court of Berdichev, there were many who objected to his appointment. The tailors and bakers especially were opposed, and they joined together and appointed a rabbi of their own choosing.

It happened that a member of the tailor and baker group was celebrating his son's *brit mila*, and he invited Rabbi Levi Yitzhak to participate in the celebration of this mitzva. The rabbi agreed to come, but on condition that the father would make a festive meal, as required by tradition. He said that in his battle against the angel Samael – Satan's prosecuting attorney, who comes down from heaven, accuses and tempts people toward transgressions, and then goes back up to heaven and prosecutes – he, Rabbi Levi Yitzhak, uses this argument:

"When a Jew fulfills a mitzva, he does so with a joyous heart. But when he stumbles and commits a transgression, his heart is broken, and this is the proof. Never have we seen a Jew, even the most non-observant, or the lowliest person, make a feast in honor of a transgression that he committed. But in honor of Shabbat and Yom Tov, or when there is an opportunity for another mitzva, such as a *brit mila*, conclusion of the study of a talmudic tractate, etc., he is happy and rejoices, and prepares a sumptuous feast in honor of the mitzva."

Rabbi Levi Yitzhak concluded by saying:

"Because of this, Samael attempts with all his might and smooth tongue to seduce the Jew not to make a feast to rejoice over a mitzva. Thus the name 'Samael,' which is an acronym for

'*Seudat Mitzva Ein Laasot*' (one should not make a *seudat mitzva*). Because of this, I am particularly strict about the father making a festive meal for the *brit*."

Jumping and Dancing

Rabbi Levi Yitzhak was a guest at the home of the Maggid of Kozhnitz (Yisroel Hopstein, d. 1814). Early in the morning, Rabbi Levi Yitzhak asked the Maggid to accompany him to the *mikve*.

The Maggid replied, "We cannot go together, because your honor walks with excitement and enthusiasm, but I walk slowly and leisurely."

Rabbi Levi Yitzhak promised to walk slowly and deliberately.

When they came close to the *mikve*, Rabbi Levi Yitzhak forgot his promise and began to dance and jump with great enthusiasm, and almost fell into the *mikve*.

Do Not Delay

"A Hasid must not be negligent in performing a mitzva,
And he should not wait for enthusiasm to come,
Because, in the meantime, the hour of the mitzva will fly by."

Moral Qualities

Know the Difference

"Searching for sins and seeking merit,
These are good moral qualities.
However, one should search for one's own sins,
But seek others' merit."

Appreciation

Rabbi Levi Yitzhak of Berdichev was visiting with the Maggid of Mezritch on the eve of Yom Kippur, when he received a letter from his father-in-law. He did not open the letter, but put it aside and said, "When Yom Kippur ends, I will read it."

After the *Ne'ila* prayer, he went to the inn where he was staying, took out the letter, and began to read: "I pay for all your needs, and therefore I ask you: Is this how you repay me? Is this the proper behavior, to forget everything and travel to Mezritch to spend months and months there?

"And is this your Torah, to repay evil for good?"

Rabbi Levi Yitzhak put down the letter and said to himself, "My father-in-law is right. But does not the Master of the world do far more good for me than my father-in-law? It is fitting, therefore, to first give thanks to the Blessed One."

He stood and recited the evening prayer.

Can It Be?

"Were the quality of arrogance not mentioned in the Torah,
I would not believe that it is found in humans,
Who are shaped out of clay.
I cannot imagine how humans can be arrogant,
When they are
All their lives as a passing shadow,
Like a fragile vessel,
Here today and gone tomorrow."

Each Generation and Its Teachers

When Rabbi Levi Yitzhak was chosen as rabbi of Berdichev, he said, "Woe unto this generation, that I am the one chosen to bring greatness to the Jewish people."

A Humble Servant on a Lowly Mountain

"When God revealed Himself to Moses at the burning bush,
And placed on his shoulders the mission to be the redeemer of
       Israel,
Moses, in his modesty, refused to accept this mission upon himself.

Why, therefore, did Moses agree at Mount Sinai immediately, with
no objection,
To accept upon himself the role of being the teacher of the Jewish people?
When Moses saw that the Blessed Holy One rejected the high
mountains as the site for giving the Torah,
And that He had chosen the smallest and lowest mountain,
Moses understood that only the lowly and humble are able to
receive the Torah.
The very quality – humility – that made Moses refuse at the burning bush, caused him to agree at Mount Sinai."

No Small Deeds

"A person must be humble in all his ways and in all his deeds, but
not, heaven forbid, when he is worshiping God.

"On the contrary, one should say, 'The deeds that I perform
in doing God's commandments are important to the Blessed Creator.' If, heaven forbid, one would be humble in performing God's
mitzvot and say, 'My deeds are not important to God,' this is heresy."

Parents and Children

Know Your Place

In one of the small villages in Poland lived an honest and righteous man. In the nearby villages he was known as Mendel the Innkeeper, as he made his living from the inn located near the main road.

When Mendel began to grow old, he thought to himself: "Most of my life has passed me by in emptiness, without meaning. I have poured drinks for inebriated gentiles and drunken barons. My eyes have witnessed the debauchery of lewd Polish landlords, and my ears have heard the wild shouts of unkempt farmers. My prayers were not proper prayers; they were rushed and half-hearted. I know only how to mumble *Shema Yisrael*. Once a year, on Yom Kippur, I prayed with the congregation, but even then I couldn't understand a word in the *maḥzor*. Now, in the twilight of my life, it's time for me to prepare for the future.

"My son, Sheike, who is now a grown man, will take care of those who come to the inn and will take charge of the inn's finances, and I will retire from my business. I shall go to the city, buy myself a *Ḥumash*, and even a new prayer book, with clear, visible letters. Like every Jew, I will pray three times a day, with concentration. And I'll try to study Torah."

Mendel summoned his son Sheike and put him in charge of the inn.

Sheike served the customers at the inn with alacrity, and the farmers continued to come in even greater numbers.

However, once Sheike took over his father's business, the inn changed. For many years, the inn had served as a hostel for travelers, for wandering Jews. When their feet gave out from exhaustion, they knew that near the highway Mendel's inn would be open for a rest stop. There would be a warm meal prepared for them, and a bed on which to stretch their weary bones. Mendel would always welcome the travelers with a smile on his face, and he would wait on them personally. With sparkling eyes, he would serve this one a warm drink, and that one a glass of spirits. But now that Mendel had left, the inn was no longer hospitable to wanderers. The little that Sheike gave to traveling Jews who happened into the inn, he gave with a sour face. Soon, travelers were no longer stopping at Mendel's inn.

When the news of the change reached Rabbi Levi Yitzhak of Berdichev, he summoned Mendel the Innkeeper. At their meeting, Rabbi Levi Yitzhak asked why Mendel had left the inn and turned it over to his son. Mendel poured out his heart to the rabbi and explained: "My hair has turned white, Rabbi. I am old, and who knows how many years the good Lord has allotted to me. With what shall I appear before the heavenly court? Will I not stand before them in embarrassment, as I have not in hand either Torah or prayer? Now that my son has assumed our livelihood, I have some leisure. I can awaken every morning, drape the tallit over my shoulders, recite each word of the prayers with feeling, and I even have some spare time to peek into the Ḥumash and the Mishna. Now, finally, I feel that I can present myself before the heavenly court with a bundle of mitzvot, including Torah and prayer."

Rabbi Levi Yitzhak sat deep in thought. After a while he turned to Mendel, and with a pleased look on his face, said quietly: "Our sages taught: 'Who is truly wise? One who knows his place.' Every Jew must recognize the place assigned to him in this world by the Creator. And he must remain in that assigned place, and not try to take the place of someone else.

"Further, our holy sages taught that the heavenly realm is just like the earthly realm. Unfortunate is the realm that has only generals, but no ordinary soldiers. A simple soldier who flees from his platoon in order to pretend to be a general is rebelling against the authorities. You should know, Mendel, that the Blessed Holy One has enough generals who are learned and privileged. What God is missing are ordinary, faithful soldiers who, in their simplicity, demonstrate their devotion. Our Creator places each of us in our proper place. God places one person in the beit midrash, and He places another in a distant village. Our Creator has placed you, Mendel, in an inn so you can serve a warm drink to tired travelers. You will stand before the gate of the Garden of Eden not as a poor man, nor will you stand before the heavenly court as one ashamed. The warm meals which you served to wanderers, and the soft beds you provided, will testify for you.

"Go, my dear Mendel, and return to your inn, and open its doors."

And so the doors of the inn that stood near the crossroads were once again opened wide, welcoming tired travelers.

Mitzvot Require *Kavana*

When Perel, wife of Rabbi Levi Yitzhak of Berdichev, would knead dough and bake *halla* for Shabbat, she would utter this prayer: "Master of the universe! May it be Your will that when my Levi

Yitzhak recites the *HaMotzi* blessing over these ḥallot, he infuse the same spiritual feeling in his heart that I have in my heart as I knead and bake them."

Three Stories

It happened that a certain person leased a parcel of land, and fell on hard times. Thus, he could not pay the landowner the rent. He left his home and traveled to a distant place to try his hand at teaching children, with the expectation that, with God's mercy, he would earn a bit of money and be able to return soon to his family and pay his debt, so that he would not have to declare bankruptcy.

One day followed another, and one year followed another, until twelve years had gone by, and he had saved up nine hundred rubles. He decided that it was time to return home to his family.

On his way home, he tarried a few days in Berdichev and prayed in the *minyan* of Rabbi Levi Yitzhak. He witnessed the tzaddik in his passion and piety, and developed a profound love toward him.

When it was time to leave, Rabbi Levi Yitzhak said to him, "I would like to relate to you three stories, on condition that his honor pay me three hundred rubles." Because of his great love for the rabbi, he agreed. He immediately removed three hundred rubles from his purse and gave them to Rabbi Levi Yitzhak. The rabbi said to him, "Now listen to my first story. You should know that anyone who sees two paths before him, and is not sure which one to take, should go to the right, as our sages of blessed memory taught: 'Each corner that you encounter, turn only to the right.'" Rabbi Levi Yitzhak continued: "But if you would like to hear my second story, you must pay me another three hundred rubles."

When he heard this, the teacher grew frightened. He had expected to pay only three hundred rubles for all three stories, and believed that six hundred rubles would be enough to discharge his debt. But what could he do with only three hundred? Yet his love for the holy tzaddik was such that he agreed to the second payment. Rabbi Levi Yitzhak said to him, "Here now is the second story. You should know that an elderly man and a young woman together are two halves of a dead person. And if you want to hear the third story, you must pay me another three hundred rubles." The teacher was horrified and almost fainted. Nevertheless, he did not dare refuse Rabbi Levi Yitzhak. He gave the matter much thought and said to himself, "Oh well, if I perish, I perish. I shall return to my home poor and penniless, and will not be able to pay my debt." He paid the last three hundred rubles.

Rabbi Levi Yitzhak said, "Now listen to the third story. Trust only what you can see with your own eyes." Rabbi Levi Yitzhak concluded, "Let his honor travel in peace, and may God bring you success in all your endeavors."

Saddened and ashamed, the teacher left Rabbi Levi Yitzhak's home, and into his heart came a gnawing thought: "Empty-handed I left my home and empty-handed I return. The rewards of my labor of twelve years I have given away for three stories. With these stories can I pay my debt, support my family, and marry off my two daughters, who were little and have now grown up?" But even in his deep sorrow he did not forget his strong love for the rabbi, from whose holy mouth came the prayers and songs which could shake entire worlds. It is clear that the love of Israel was in his heart, and surely he did not intend to cause him any harm, or steal the fruit of his labor. Thinking this, he was comforted, as it seemed there was some underlying reason for what had happened. Not for naught did the tzaddik take all his assets from him.

The poor teacher traveled on foot, since he had not a cent to part with. He walked and walked, and his thoughts wandered with him. What would he do now? How could he cross the threshold of his home and face his family with empty pockets? How would he explain what had happened to his earnings of all those years? Should he tell them that robbers attacked him on the way, and left him penniless? Or, perhaps, he should not return home just now, and instead find another position as a teacher near his home, until God had mercy upon him and he could accumulate a little money once again.

On the way, he noticed some men running, chasing someone. When they saw him they asked him if he had passed a man running away, a thief, who stole all their money. Had he noticed which way the thief had run? Even though he had not seen the thief, he advised the men giving chase to turn to the right. And so they did. They ran to the right, and he ran with them. They caught the thief, who had all the money, amounting to thousands of rubles. They immediately removed six hundred rubles and gave them as a gift to their excellent guide who had rescued all their money.

Since his pockets were no longer empty and it had begun to get dark, he decided he would repair to an inn. He approached an inn and there he saw an elderly man and his young wife who managed the inn. He asked for a room and the elderly gentleman agreed. However, the young woman chased him away with a growl. He left to try to find another inn. Unfortunately, he could not. He decided to go back to the inn and knock once more on the door. And if they would not let him in, he would lie down outside under a nearby tree. He went and knocked on the door. The young woman came out and chased him away, cursing in anger and calling him a thief. He accepted his fate.

The door closed in his face with a loud crash, and he lay down under the tree, eyes closed. He could not sleep. A light rain began to fall, but the leaves of the tree protected him, just as darkness concealed him from the eyes of the evil woman. A short while later, he heard the noise of an approaching wagon. Then he heard whispering between the two people who got off the wagon and the woman, who had opened the door for them.

He listened carefully to their whispered conversation, and blanched. It seemed that they were talking about the old man, conspiring, he guessed, a murder. He remembered the words of Rabbi Levi Yitzhak, that an old man and a young woman were two halves of a dead person. He waited a little while and then began to bang on the inn door, screaming loudly, until the would-be murderers fled. He entered the inn and saw that the elderly man was lying with his feet tied, alone, since his wife had escaped with the others. He untied the old man and explained what had occurred. The old man hugged him, and with tears streaming from his eyes asked, "How can I repay you? You saved my life! Name your fee and it's yours!" The teacher answered, "Please give me three hundred rubles." The old man paid him in hard cash. Tears of joy and appreciation streamed from his eyes.

Now he had completely restored his savings of nine hundred rubles. The next day he returned home with a merry heart. However, before he went into the house he inquired of the neighbors about the situation of his family. The neighbors, who did not recognize him, related to him that his wife had become a loose woman, God should spare her. The teacher remembered what Rabbi Levi Yitzhak had told him about believing only what he saw with his own eyes. He dressed himself in old clothes and at night, under the cover of darkness, lay down near his house. He saw a young man knock on the door and go inside. He waited for dawn, and saw the young man sneaking away from the house. The teacher's heart thumped. But he overcame his sadness and fear when he remembered the words of Rabbi Levi Yitzhak.

The next day, he went to the village inn to rest from the travails of his journey. He washed, donned his best clothes, and went to his house. His wife immediately recognized him and received him with great joy. She told him everything that happened from the day he had left her alone in the village, where she had no friends. She was left with her two daughters, after their six-year-old boy had been snatched by the Polish landlord, who was holding him until the repayment of their debt. She had suffered terribly during his absence. Thank God, however, she sees her husband alive. Their two daughters are grown, and, thank God, they are already engaged, and their wedding dates have already been set.

"So, my dear husband," she said, "you have arrived on a blessed day; 'This is all from the Lord' (Ps. 118)." She concluded with a sigh, "Woe unto us because of our poor son. God blessed us with a fine son, a precious child. He has not abandoned, heaven forbid, the faith of his ancestors, and he is faithful in his heart to our tradition. On occasion, at night, when no one is in sight, he comes to me and I teach him some of the prayers in the siddur.

"I hoped and prayed that you would return and redeem your son... and here you are!"

"Yes," rejoiced the husband, "and here is the bundle of money with which we can redeem him."

Passover

Day Laborers

Rabbi Levi Yitzhak of Berdichev once walked around to visit the local bakeries before Passover. He not only inspected the *kashrut* in baking the matza, but also checked to see that the bakery owners would not overwork the women and children day laborers.

When he saw that in one bakery the owner was exploiting the women and children, forcing them to work from early morning until late in the evening, he said to him:

"Anti-Semites libeled against us that we bake matza with Christian blood, heaven forbid. But God knows, and you all know, that this libel is an abominable lie and a ridiculous rumor. However, to my great sorrow, I see that there are bakers who use Jewish blood, the blood of unfortunate Jewish children; bakers who, woe unto us, suck from them their last measure of strength!"

In Vain the Guardian Perseveres

One Passover eve, Rabbi Levi Yitzhak of Berdichev took a walk with his servant in the streets of the city. He encountered a certain gentile, one of those who smuggle contraband, and asked him:

"Do you have illegal merchandise that was brought from across the border?"

"Of course. Please come with me. I have a great deal of such illegal merchandise in my home."

Rabbi Levi Yitzhak ignored him and continued on his way. Then he encountered a Jew and asked him:

"Is it possible that you have leavened bread in your home?"

"Now?" replied the Jew in astonishment. "It's the afternoon of Passover eve!"

Rabbi Levi Yitzhak met another Jew and asked the same question.

"Rabbi, do you take me for a fool, or are you suspicious of a kosher Jew? It's already past the time for burning and nullifying unleavened bread."

Rabbi Levi Yitzhak lifted his eyes to heaven and said:

"Master of the universe! Look down from Your holy habitation, and consider Your people Israel, how faithfully they follow Your commandments. The Czar of Russia is a powerful ruler. How many judges and police has he stationed, how many soldiers and guards has he posted in every corner of the country and in every border city, and they all carefully defend the laws and supervise the borders so that no one can smuggle merchandise without paying tax. And with it all, people openly violate the law.

"And You, Master of the universe, wrote in Your Torah, 'No leavened bread will be found in your homes' (Ex. 13:7). You did not post police or guards or border patrols, and on Passover eve, no leavened bread is found in a Jewish home!"

"These My Heart Desires"

At the conclusion of the festivals – Passover and Sukkot – Rabbi Levi Yitzhak would stay awake all night, awaiting the dawn, so that he could hurry and wrap his tefillin, since eight days had passed since he last put them on.

He would say: "My hand yearns for tefillin, and my head deeply desires them."

Why, Oh Why?

When Rabbi Levi Yitzhak of Berdichev reached the section of the Haggada which deals with the "Four Sons," of which the fourth was "Who does know how to ask," he would say:

"That's me, Levi Yitzhak of Berdichev. I do not know how to ask You, Master of the universe, and if I knew, would I dare to ask? How would I dare to ask You, Master of the universe, why has all this come upon us. Why are we chased from exile to exile? Why are our enemies permitted to oppress us so much?

"But in the Passover Haggada it says: The one who does not know how to ask – you start him off, as it is written, 'You shall tell your son.' And I, Master of the universe, I am Your son, I do not ask You to reveal to me the mysteries of Your ways. For that, my understanding is limited. But please, You start, and tell me: What is the reason for the horrible things that are happening now? What do they require of me? What are You trying to tell me? I do not want to know why I suffer. I just want to know if I am suffering for Your name."

As Long As the Heart Is Directed Heavenward

It happened once that Rabbi Levi Yitzhak of Berdichev was leading the Passover Seder on the first evening of the holiday, following all the rules meticulously, so that every commandment and every custom shone on the tzaddik's table with its hidden meaning. At the end of the Seder, at dawn, he sat in his room, pleased that the Seder had gone so well.

Suddenly, he heard a voice: "What are you so proud of? The Seder of Hayim the water carrier is more pleasing to Me than yours."

The rabbi called together his family and his students and asked about this man. But no one knew a thing.

Immediately, the tzaddik sent some of his students to find him. For a long while they wandered through the streets, and finally arrived at the poor neighborhood at the edge of the city. There they were pointed to the house of Hayim the water carrier.

The students knocked on the door and a woman came out and asked what they wanted. When she heard the story, she was surprised and said, "Yes, Hayim the water carrier is my husband. However, he cannot go with you, since he drank a lot last night and he is now sleeping. And even if I would awaken him, he would not be able to lift his legs."

The students answered, "The rabbi ordered us to bring him." They entered his room and shook him. He stared at them with clouded eyes and did not understand what they wanted from him. He just wanted to go back to sleep. They immediately lifted him out of bed, held him up by his arms, and practically carried him on their shoulders to the tzaddik.

The rabbi ordered a chair brought next to him, and as the water carrier sat silent and confused the tzaddik leaned over to him and said, "My dear Reb Hayim, what is the hidden meaning you pondered as you searched for leavened bread?" The water carrier looked at him with wondering eyes, shook his head, and answered, "Rabbi, I searched in every corner and gathered the crumbs of leavened bread into the spoon." The tzaddik asked again in surprise, "And what meditation did you ponder when you burned the leavened bread?" The man thought to himself, and answered in embarrassment, "Rabbi, I forgot to burn the leavened bread, and I just remembered that it is still lying under the beam in my house."

When Rabbi Levi Yitzhak heard this, he began to have doubts, but asked again, "So now, please tell me, Reb Hayim, how did you lead the Seder?" Suddenly it seemed as if a spark lit up in his eyes, and he answered in a humble voice: "Rabbi, I will not hide the truth from your honor. I heard that it is forbidden to drink brandy during all eight days of the festival of Passover, therefore I drank yesterday morning enough to last me the whole holiday, and I became tired and slept. My wife awakened me and said, 'Why are you not arranging the Seder, as all Jews do?' I replied, 'What do you want, and what are you asking of me? I am a simple, ignorant man. My father was also a boor, and I do not know what I am supposed to do or what is forbidden to do, and how to arrange a Passover Seder according to Jewish law. But this much I know. Our forefathers were captives under the control of vagabonds, and we have a God in heaven who brought us out from slavery to freedom. And look, here we are again captives, and I know clearly and say to you that the Blessed Holy One will take us out again to freedom.'

"Then I saw the table set, and on it was set out a gleaming white tablecloth, and on the table were dishes of matza, eggs, and other foods, and a bottle of red wine. So I ate the matza and the eggs, and I drank some wine, and I gave my wife some food and wine. Then I was overcome with joy, and I lifted my glass toward heaven and said: 'See, God, I make this toast to You! Now bring Yourself down to us and redeem us!' Thus we ate and drank and rejoiced before the Creator, and afterward I became tired, so I lay down and fell asleep."

Rabbi Levi Yitzhak heard these words and ordered his students to escort the water carrier to his house. After he left, the tzaddik said to his followers: "The words of Reb Hayim were most pleasing to God, since he said them in truth, with no selfish motive, in total sincerity and honest intentions, for he knows only those."

"For I am Sick with Love"

When Rabbi Levi Yitzhak would eat the required amount of *maror* at the Seder, he would always be very sad, and sigh profusely.

His friends reported that when he ate it, he would feel and sense all the pain and sorrow of the People of Israel in Egypt.

The Key to the Heart Is in Our Hands

It happened once that Rabbi Levi Yitzhak of Berdichev said to one of his students on the night of the Seder, just before the recitation of "Pour out Your wrath," "Go open the door!"

The student ran in haste, delighted that his rabbi chose him to open the door for Elijah the prophet.

The tzaddik sensed this and said to him, "You are mistaken. Elijah the prophet does not come through the door. He comes through the mind and the heart."

Prayer

The Spirit of Tears

"Poems and songs
Are created by the masters of language and flowery phrases.
But later, when they are soaked
With the tears of Jews,
They are transformed into *Seliḥot*."

He Listens to the Prayer of Every Mouth

It happened once that Rabbi Levi Yitzhak of Berdichev was traveling, and he stayed overnight at a certain inn. At the same inn there were some Jewish merchants on their way to a fair. These merchants were not acquainted with Rabbi Levi Yitzhak, and he appeared to them as just one of the passersby.

The next day, the merchants arose early. Since they had only one pair of tefillin, they quickly passed the tefillin around, and recited hurried prayers in their haste to reach the fair.

When they had completed their prayers, Rabbi Levi Yitzhak turned to two of them, among the youngest in the group, and said, "If you please, come here. I have a question for you."

They approached him, and he began to mumble, "*Ma, ma, ma. Na, na, na.*"

"What are you saying?" asked the merchants. Rabbi Levi Yitzhak continued to mumble, "*Ba, ba, ba. Ta, ta, ta.*"

The merchants stared at him in amazement. This man must have lost his mind.

"Really?" asked Rabbi Levi Yitzhak, as though he were also amazed. "Do you not understand what I am saying? But this is the same way that you just spoke to God!"

"Do not worry," answered one of the merchants. "Let me explain with this analogy. A baby lying in his crib mumbles, 'ba, ma, da.' If all the wise men of the East and West gathered, they would not understand what the baby is saying. But if his parents passed by and heard him, they would immediately know what he wanted, if he is hungry or thirsty.

"So it is with us, the People of Israel. We are the children of God, and He knows the desires of every heart, and listens to the prayers of every mouth."

"Well said," Rabbi Levi Yitzhak exclaimed, jumping for joy. "Our Father in heaven listens to the prayers of His children."

❧ ❧ ❧

Shalom Aleikhem

It happened once that Rabbi Levi Yitzhak approached a group of Hasidim who had just finished the recitation of the *Shemoneh Esreh*, shook their hands, and blessed them warmly: "*Shalom Aleikhem!*"

The Hasidim were surprised, since they had not left the city on a trip and just returned, and they were not strangers who had come to the city from nearby.

When Rabbi Levi Yitzhak saw their surprise, he said to them, "Why are you surprised? From the expression on your faces, I can see that you were in a faraway place, correct? You were in a wheat market in Odessa, or in a wool market in Lodz, or perhaps you were on a remote ship sailing to a port in some commercial city. There is no doubt when the sound of your prayers quietened, that you returned from some far-off place. Therefore, *Shalom Aleikhem*."

The Time of Prayer

Rabbi Avraham Katzenelbogen of Brisk asked Rabbi Levi Yitzhak:
"Why do the Hasidim miss the correct time of *Keriat Shema* and *Shemoneh Esreh*?"

Rabbi Levi Yitzhak replied: "My dear rabbi of Brisk, we never heard that there is a clock in heaven, with angels standing near and looking at the hands of the clock in order to determine the exact time of the prayers.

"I, Levi Yitzhak, am of the opinion that every Jew is obligated at all times to arise and announce that we have one God, and to worship Him always, and not necessarily according to the instructions of the keeper of the clock."

One Who Knows Our Thoughts

It happened once at the end of Yom Kippur that Rabbi Levi Yitzhak said to one of the worshipers in the beit midrash:
"I will tell you what you prayed for today. First, you asked of the Blessed One that He arrange for you one thousand rubles in cash, so that you will be able to study Torah comfortably.

"Then you changed your mind and said that if you acquire a thousand rubles all at once, you would open a store and be very busy with it, and against your will you would neglect your Torah study. So you requested from the Blessed One to divide the amount into two parts.

"And then during the *Ne'ila* prayer, an idea came into your head that it is arrogant to request of the Blessed One two large sums, one after another. You agreed to accept from the Master of the universe the sum of rubles in four installments, two hundred and fifty rubles every three months, so that you would be able to study Torah in a relaxed state of mind.

"It is a wonder to me that it never occurred to you that perhaps the Blessed Holy One is not at all interested in your Torah study, but be busy and preoccupied and worried."

‿‿ ‿‿ ‿‿

One Prayer Does Not Resemble Another

It happened once that Rabbi Levi Yitzhak was visiting a distant city, and when he went to the synagogue on Friday night he led the prayers. As was his practice, he added several cries and motions that were not customary, and that lengthened the service considerably.

When he concluded his prayers, the rabbi of the city approached him, wished him "*Shabbat Shalom*," and asked: "Why did you so extend the service, and not concern yourself with the inconvenience to the congregation? Is it not written in the Talmud, 'It was the custom of Rabbi Akiva, when he prayed with the community, he would be brief and finish so as not to inconvenience the congregation, but when he would pray alone, one could leave him in one corner and find him later in another, on account of his many genuflections and prostrations' (Berakhot 31a)?"

Rabbi Levi Yitzhak replied: "Is it possible to think that Rabbi Akiva, with his thousands of students, would shorten his prayers in order not to inconvenience the congregation? Surely every one of them would wait happily hour after hour for the sake of his rabbi.

"Rather, the intent of the Talmud is this: When Rabbi Akiva prayed with the congregation fully, namely, when the congregation directed their hearts in prayer as did Rabbi Akiva, he permitted himself to cut short the worship, since he only had to pray for himself. But when he would pray alone, namely, even though he was praying in the midst of the congregation – but the community was not directing its heart during prayer – then he alone would be praying with intention, while the rest were praying without intention. Against his will, he would lengthen his prayer, and with it raise their prayers to a higher level."

Yesterday and Today

Rabbi Levi Yitzhak taught:

We live in an upside down world.

It used to be that among Jews, absolute truth was prevalent in the streets and in the markets, and everyone spoke the truth. But when they came to the synagogue, there was no fear of speaking lies. But now, everything is reversed. In the streets and in the city squares they all speak lies, but in the synagogue, they declare the truth.

Because in the past this was the custom among Jews: truth and honesty were guiding principles. And when they went to the market and to the world of business, they would affirm in their soul the saying, "Let your Yes be Yes, and your No be No," and all their business transactions were honest.

But when they went to the synagogue, they would beat their hearts and say, "We are guilty, we are rebellious, we have stolen," and it was all false, because they were faithful with God and people.

Today it is backward. In their business dealings they lie and cheat, and in the synagogue they declare the truth.

Requests Pour Forth

A certain Hasid stayed overnight with Rabbi Levi Yitzhak of Berdichev and said to him:

"Rabbi, I noticed today several people who came here and brought your honor notes with prayers and requests. People come and go, all with their individual worries and problems. How can your honor, with his prayers, help all the troubled souls? How can you possibly remember each person's request?"

Rabbi Levi Yitzhak replied:

"Truthfully, I cannot remember, but every request and appeal of every Jew is engraved on my heart because of the infinite compassion I have for our brothers and sisters, the People of Israel. When I stand and pray, and pour out my heart like water before the Blessed One, out of my heart flow the requests and prayers of all those who come to me and cry for help."

The Source of Hoarseness

"Why is your voice hoarse?" asked Rabbi Levi Yitzhak of Berdichev of a certain cantor.

"Because I prayed before the ark," answered the cantor.

"True," replied Rabbi Levi Yitzhak, "whoever prays before the ark, his voice becomes hoarse. But one who prays before the Blessed Holy One, his voice does not become hoarse."

Compensation

"Master of the universe," exclaimed Rabbi Levi Yitzhak of Berdichev, "is it not a law that one who injures another must compensate for five categories of injury: damage, pain, medical costs, inability to work, shame? Therefore, what is the compensation to us for all our suffering and torment?

"If You argue that You are exempt from the payment of medical costs, since You are injuring Your own children, the law is that one who harms his children, and they are not dependent upon him, is liable! And if You want to argue that the requirement to pay medical costs does not apply to You, since it is written, 'I am the Lord, who heals you' – namely that You Yourself are the Healer – does the Talmud not say that if the one who injures is the healer, he may not exempt himself (Bava Kamma 85a)?

"Why then, Master of the universe, do You not comply with the law? Why do You not compensate us for our terrible suffering?"

That We Should Not Need One Another

Rabbi Levi Yitzhak asked the following question:

"We pray that 'we should not have to rely on each other, or upon another nation.' Why should we care if a gentile purchases something from a Jew, allowing him to earn an honorable living? What is the purpose of this prayer?"

He asked, and he answered:

"If someone is guilty by decision of the heavenly court, what does the defender do? He brings a 'worse' Jew as an example and argues: the convicted is a tzaddik compared to the other person, so why do you declare him guilty?

"If there is no greater sinner than the defendant, the defender brings a gentile and compares him to the guilty Jew. That is the meaning of the prayer: Let all Jews be tzaddikim, so they will not need to be compared to another Jew or to a gentile."

Introduction to *Seliḥot* Prayers

Once Rabbi Levi Yitzhak introduced the *Seliḥot* prayers with these words:

"Master of the universe, who am I, what am I, flesh and blood, very frail. I do not have the strength to stand all night long with requests for forgiveness from You.

"But You are the living God, strong and mighty. With You there is no old age, You do not sleep, and it is not difficult for You to recite *Seliḥot* for our sake.

"You do not have to elaborate, just answer and say these words: 'I forgive.'"

Prayer before *Havdala*

Thus would Rabbi Levi Yitzhak say:

God of Abraham, God of Isaac, God of Jacob, protect Your people Israel from all evil, for the sake of Your name and Your glory.

Behold the holy Sabbath is waning.

May it be Your will that the coming week will be for complete faith, faith of the wise, love of friends, and clinging to the Blessed Creator; to believe in Your thirteen principles, and in the coming redemption, speedily in our day, in the resurrection of the dead, and in the prophecy of Moses, may he rest in peace.

Master of the universe, You give strength to the weary; please give to our brothers and sisters, your beloved People of Israel, strength to thank and praise You, and to worship You alone.

May the week to come bring us good health, good luck, success, blessing, and loving-kindness, long life, livelihood for us and all Israel – and let us say, Amen!

Then Sang Moses

"Let me sing to You now, Master of the universe, the song of 'You.'
Wherever I go – You are there, and wherever I stand – You are there.
Only You, again You, forever You.
If things are good for me – You, and if things are not good for me,
    heaven forbid – You.
Only You, again You, forever You.
Heaven – You, earth – You,
Above – You, below – You.
Wherever I look and whatever I see – You.
Only You, again You, forever You."

The Gates of Prayer

When Rabbi Levi Yitzhak passed away, there was a certain tzaddik living in a distant city who was lecturing to his students, and wanted to combine the power of Torah with the power of prayer.

Suddenly, he stopped and said, "I can speak no further. My eyes grow dim. Certainly something has happened to the great intercessor, Rabbi Levi Yitzhak."

The Vision

Rabbi Levi Yitzhak once saw a vision, and heard a heavenly voice announcing: "Be strong, Levi Yitzhak My son, be strong. You should know, Levi Yitzhak, that terrible troubles will befall you. But do not be afraid, since I am with you."

And so it was. Rabbi Levi Yitzhak arrived at a nearby city on a very dark night, and could not find anyone to host him. Rabbi Levi Yitzhak was dispirited, until the Blessed One took pity on him and a leather merchant passed by and invited him to stay for the night. The rabbi wanted to recite the evening prayer, but he did not have enough peace of mind. And the merchant was a crude, unsavory character, who did not see to his guest.

Rabbi Levi Yitzhak went outside alone in the dark, and saw a sliver of light shining in the distance. He recognized that it was a beit midrash. He entered, but no one was there. He stood there alone and recited prayers until midnight, and cried bitterly and said:

"Levi Yitzhak, go outside and look at your pitiful state on this dark night, and you will understand how great is the pain of the *Shekhina* in exile, standing like you in the dark exile, and looking for a leather merchant who will take her into his home."

As he was saying this, Rabbi Levi Yitzhak broke out in bitter crying, and due to his terrible agony and crying he fell asleep. In his dream, he saw a vision of a shining light, adorned with twenty-four ornaments. It darkened the brightness of the sun, and he heard a voice saying: "Be strong, be strong, My son."

Rabbi Levi Yitzhak cried, and asked: "Why do I not merit
seeing the face of the *Shekhina*?"
The heavenly voice replied: "You are flesh and blood, and it
is written 'No human will see me and live' (Ex. 33:20)."

Leader of Prayer

"The tzaddik, when he prays before the Blessed One,
Must connect himself to the words of the prayers,
And the holy words, they lead him.
And there are great tzaddikim who surpass this level,
And they lead the words."

Purim

Physical and Spiritual Destruction

"Why did the rabbis determine that the miracle of Purim be commemorated with joy and feasting, but the miracle of Hanukka be commemorated with prayers of thanksgiving and praise?

"Because the decree of the wicked Haman was 'to destroy, to kill, and wipe out all the Jews' – i.e., physical destruction. The miracle, thus, was seen as a sign of physical salvation for the Jews, to be celebrated by days of 'joy and feasting' for the body.

"In the days of the Hasmoneans, the decree was about the Torah of Israel, and the belief in the God of Israel, 'to turn them away from the laws which You desire.'

"In this miracle, therefore, we see salvation of the spirit and the Torah of Israel, for which we give thanks and praise."

You Shall Meditate on Them Day and Night

The father of Rabbi Levi Yitzhak of Berdichev was asked, "For what reason did you merit such a precious son?"

He replied, "When the Jewish people were occupied during Purim with 'One must drink abundantly on Purim,' I always found time to study Torah, so that the study of Torah in Israel would not cease, heaven forbid, for so much as a minute."

Rabbi and Leader

From My Own Personal Experience

Rabbi Levi Yitzhak used to tell this story:

When I noticed that the people of my city were not listening to me, I began to examine my deeds. Then I noticed that even my own family were not respecting me. I investigated further, and the Blessed One enlightened me to understand that the fault lay within me, since I myself was not conducting myself properly.

I tried to improve myself.

When my family noticed that I was working hard to improve myself, they began to obey me, and the citizens of my city also stopped rebelling and no longer refused to accept my opinions.

The Bridal Gown

The bridal gown of a young bride was stolen from her home close to the wedding date. The father of the bride poured out his sorrow to Rabbi Levi Yitzhak and the rabbi promised him that, with God's help, he would find the thief and have him return it.

Immediately, Rabbi Levi Yitzhak brought together his judges, sat them down for a tribunal with the Blessed Holy One, and presented his case: "The Master of the universe is surely obligated to fulfill what is written in His Torah, 'You shall not steal.' Whoever stole the bridal gown is obligated to return what was stolen. To whom does the world belong? It belongs to the Blessed Holy One – 'there is no place empty of Him.' It is obvious that the stolen bridal gown is some place, and every place is God's, since God is everywhere. From this we learn that the stolen gown is in the possession, heaven forbid, of the Blessed Creator, and He is obligated to return it to its rightful owner."

The judges listened to the claim and transcribed it on paper word for word as it emerged from the holy mouth of Rabbi Levi Yitzhak.

Rabbi Levi Yitzhak argued further:

"It is well known that every monarchy before which one brings a case of thievery, it is not sufficient that it appoint judges to judge the thief, but it must also appoint messengers to inspect hidden corners, nooks, and crannies, and to search for the stolen property. But the Blessed Holy One, who is Omnipotent and Omniscient, does not need special messengers and expert officials to dig for treasure and find the stolen objects. He can put forth His hand and bang with a hammer on the hearts of the thieves, until they are struck with pangs of conscience for having taken property that didn't belong to them. He can also create ears for those deaf to the cries of oppressed poor people who are victims of thievery, so that they can hear and tremble at the oppression caused by their evil actions, repent, and return the stolen property to its rightful owner. And if this can happen to every thief, how much more so to this cruel thief who took the bridal gown of an upright Jewish woman, and robbed her of her pride and joy for her wedding day.

"Is it possible that there exists such a Jew with a heart so cruel that he would deprive the joy from a bride and groom as they are about to build a Jewish home? And if there is such a Jew, strike his heart, Master of the universe, beat him with Your hammer, so that he is aroused to repent."

These last words of Rabbi Levi Yitzhak were shouted out with a searing, bitter cry. And some say that Rabbi Levi Yitzhak broke out crying. When the details of the judgment were heard in the city, there was great clamor, and even the thieves were frightened.

That very night, three men, a Jew and two gentiles, knocked on the door of the father of the bride and returned the bridal gown, which had been placed in a large trunk. The Jew handed him the trunk quietly. But the two gentiles told this story: "At night we dug a deep hole in the forest and inside we hid the trunk. The next day, early in the morning, when we came to the place in the forest where we had buried the trunk, we noticed that the trunk was on the ground. We were very frightened. We looked further and saw that the heavy trunk was moving, as if it were floating in the air. We were frightened lest you are a witch, and if so, here is your trunk."

They Chased Me in Vain

Rabbi Levi Yitzhak of Berdichev experienced many insults and persecution in all the cities where he served as chief rabbi.

One of them was the village of Zhilikhov. There, the harassment reached such a point that one day, as Rabbi Levi Yitzhak was strolling in the street, the wife of the head of the community emptied a jug of waste water on his head, and abused and taunted him with no end of curses and insults.

Rabbi Levi Yitzhak ran to the beit midrash, stood before the holy ark, stretched his hands upward, and prayed: "Please, Master of the universe, do not punish this woman, since our holy sages taught, 'Who is an upright woman? Whoever does the will of her husband' (*Tanna DeVei Eliyahu Rabba* 9). So too is this woman upright – she did the will of her husband, since it is clear that he ordered her to do this."

As is known, Rabbi Levi Yitzhak left Zhilikhov in the middle of Hoshana Rabba.

➳ ➳ ➳

Forgiveness

When Rabbi Levi Yitzhak was appointed rabbi of Berdichev, the head of the community and some of his colleagues strenuously objected. And since the head of the community was close to the gentile government leaders in Berdichev, he used these connections to try to limit the influence of the new rabbi.

On a certain Friday, when Rabbi Levi Yitzhak was out of town, the head of the community brought a garbage wagon to the rabbi's house, forced the rabbi's wife and small children into it, and sent them, humiliated, out of the city.

This cruel act by the community head caused a storm of protest in the city, and the rabbi's followers gathered on Saturday night to decide on an appropriate response to this vulgar tyrant. Inter alia, several friends of Rabbi Levi Yitzhak traveled to the city of Zhitomir to get advice from Rabbi Zev Wolf (author of *Or HaMe'ir*, a leading student of the Maggid of Mezritch), who was a close friend and admirer of their great rabbi.

Rabbi Zev Wolf sat with the guests from Berdichev for a long time. The guests recounted all the evil deeds of the head of the community in Berdichev, who had aggressively and arrogantly tormented their righteous rabbi. Amidst this storm of words, one of the elders of Berdichev turned to Rabbi Zev Wolf with a plea that he offer a prayer to heaven that this evildoer be swiftly punished.

Rabbi Zev Wolf smiled and replied, "I would be happy to comply with your request, and recite such a prayer. I am certain though that Rabbi Levi Yitzhak is already praying for him." When he saw the surprised looks on the faces of the guests from Berdichev, Rabbi Zev Wolf continued: "While we are here discussing how to hasten the overthrow of the evil leader in Berdichev, surely Rabbi Levi Yitzhak is already reciting from his book of Psalms, and pleading for mercy from the Blessed One, to curb His anger at the head of the community and his henchmen, and to save them from all trouble and misfortune."

ℜosh HaShana

Please

"Master of the universe!
You said to us, 'You shall observe it as a day when the horn is sounded' (Num. 29:1).
Because of this one command, we sound 'one hundred blasts,' for
    thousands of years,
Blown by many thousands of Jews.
And we, tens of thousands of Jews, cry out and pray
And plead unto You these many thousands of years:
Please, 'Sound the great shofar to signal our freedom,'
One single blast.
So why have You still not sounded the great shofar?!"

Saving a Life

Once, when Rosh HaShana fell on Shabbat, Rabbi Levi Yitzhak
of Berdichev petitioned God:
"Master of the universe! On this Rosh HaShana You are
obliged according to Jewish law to inscribe all of the People of

Israel for a good life and for peace. After all, today is the holy Shabbat, and writing is forbidden. It is impossible to fulfill the words of the prayer, 'On Rosh HaShana it is written.'

"But, if you inscribe us in Your book for life, You are permitted to write, since saving a life overrules observance of Shabbat."

᠀᠀᠀

Fire and Water

Rabbi Levi Yitzhak of Berdichev told this story:

"Some young soldiers who served in the days of Czar Nicholas of Russia (d. 1855), after they were kidnapped from their parents' homes and sent to faraway regions, gathered together in hiding on Rosh HaShana.

"One of the youngsters said, 'Jews, come let us pray to God on this great, awesome day.'

"To his great sorrow, no one remembered a single prayer by heart.

"Another youngster added, 'Jews, on Rosh HaShana we not only pray, we also recite Psalms. Does any of you remember a chapter of Psalms?'

"Not one of them remembered a chapter of Psalms.

"A third youngster added, 'I don't remember by heart any chapter of Psalms, but I remember the melody for the Psalms.' The young man burst forth with the melody of Psalms, and everyone joined in. The melody was accompanied by much weeping."

Rabbi Levi Yitzhak concluded, "The strength of that melody, which was as powerful as many prayers, even those of fiery passion, shook the entire heavenly host."

When one tzaddik heard this moving story, he added his own perspective, saying, "There is an aspect of fiery passion, and there is an aspect of flowing, cleansing tears. The power of the latter is greater than that of the former. Water extinguishes fire, but fire does not burn water. Opposed to holy fire is foreign fire. But water is pure, and always purifies."

A Day of Remembrance

Once, before the blowing of the shofar on Rosh HaShana, Rabbi Levi Yitzhak stood up before the congregation and related this allegory:

"A certain king went to the forest to hunt, and after going deep into the forest he lost his way and could not find the way back home. Weeks and months passed, and the people of the country searched and searched, until finally they despaired of ever finding him. The time passed and little by little, they began to turn their attention away from the king and to forget him, but he was still lost in the forest and could not find his way back.

"One day, the forest watchman saw a man walking around, lost. He looked him in the face and immediately recognized that it was the king. With great joy, he set the king on the right path and accompanied him to his city and his home.

"The country's officers had already forgotten their king, but the forest watchman proved to them that he was their king, who had been lost in the forest for a long time and could not find his way out. The officers hurried to restore the king to his position, and returned him to the throne with much honor and glory. As a sign of appreciation to the watchman, the king appointed him an honored officer.

"Some time later, this officer committed a serious transgression, and the king's council sentenced him to death. As they led him to the gallows, his final request was that they clothe him in his former uniform, when he was guardian of the forest, and place the hanging post in view of the king's window.

"His request was fulfilled, and when the king saw, through the window, the hanging post and the guardian of the forest in his former uniform, his heart filled with great pity. He remembered the time that he himself was a wanderer, roaming in the depths of the terrible forest, and only this man, the guardian, recognized him, and only to him was the king indebted for being king and returned to his royal throne, and to ruling the country. At that moment, the king tore up the decree, pardoned the guardian for his transgression, and returned him to his former honored position.

"We too," concluded Rabbi Levi Yitzhak, "with the blasts of the shofar today, remind the Master of the universe that we were the first, when we heard the sound of the shofar at Mount Sinai, to immediately recognize the King, and proclaim His kingdom throughout the world, among all peoples throughout every land, where the name of the Blessed Holy One was completely forgotten.

"Therefore, we have the merit to demand that He forget our transgressions, and treat us leniently, beyond the letter of the law. And so, dear Jews, let us begin the psalm that precedes the shofar blasts: 'Hear this, all you peoples, give ear, all inhabitants of the world' (Ps. 49:2)."

≥● ≥● ≥●

Prayer Before Blowing of the Shofar

"Master of the universe,
> What do You think? That I will blow the shofar before You on this
>> Rosh HaShana too?
> Let the evil kingdom make their sound before You, the one that
>> afflicts us with harsh decrees.

But what shall I do, Master of the world, as I love You with eternal love?

Therefore I will nullify my will in favor of Your will, and nevertheless I shall recite, '*Tekia!*'"

Devotion

As Rosh HaShana approached, Rabbi Levi Yitzhak sought a *baal toke'a* for his synagogue. Expert shofar blowers streamed to him from all corners of the city. Many skilled blowers ran to him, wishing for this special privilege of blowing the shofar in the synagogue of the rabbi.

Rabbi Levi Yitzhak tested each one and asked, "What is your inner feeling when you blow the shofar?"

Each of the candidates attempted to show his strength in intent and special meditations on God's oneness, passed down by the Ari (Rabbi Yitzhak Luria) and other great kabbalists, that are known only to those who share secret wisdom.

Rabbi Levi Yitzhak was not satisfied with any of them.

One day, a *baal toke'a* approached the rabbi and said, "My master, I am the simplest of simple men. I have four daughters, and they all have reached maturity, but I do not have enough funds to arrange weddings for them. So here is my *kavana* when I blow the shofar: 'Master of the universe, I have bent my will to Your will and I have fulfilled the mitzvot. Now it is Your turn to bend Your will to my will, and find partners for my daughters.'"

Rabbi Levi Yitzhak was filled with great joy and said to him, "Your devotion is sincere. You will blow the shofar in my synagogue."

The Blessed Holy One Joins Prayers Together

Rabbi Levi Yitzhak of Berdichev himself used to serve as the *baal toke'a* on Rosh HaShana. It happened once, before the *tekiot*, that Rabbi Levi Yitzhak donned his *kittel*, draped himself in his tallit, and ascended the pulpit. He recited the psalm *"LaMenatze'aḥ"* seven times, and the psalm *"Min HaMetzar"* three times, as is the custom, and took the shofar in hand. But he was silent. He put the shofar down, again picked it up, and again put it down. The congregation stood with their tallitot wrapped around their heads, waiting in awe and anticipation – but they heard nary a blessing or shofar blast.

A deep, eerie silence reigned in the beit midrash, and then Rabbi Levi Yitzhak turned to the congregation and said: "My friends, next to the doorway sits a gentleman who lived most of his years among gentiles, and, poor thing, does not know how to pray. Out of his great sorrow that he does not know how to pray with the community, this Jew began to cry and said to the Master of the universe: 'I am an ignorant man. I do not know how to pray, and You, Master of the universe, You know all the true intentions of all the prayers, and You understand the full truth. And because I do not know more than the *aleph-bet*, I ask of You, I will recite before You, *aleph, bet, gimmel, dalet…* and You please create, from the letters, prayers.'

"Now," concluded Rabbi Levi Yitzhak, "the Blessed Holy One, as it were, is building prayers from the *aleph-bet* of this Jew. Therefore, it seems appropriate for us to wait a bit."

The Last Shofar Blast

On the very last Rosh HaShana of Rabbi Levi Yitzhak's life, no one succeeded in blowing the shofar. No one could manage to bring a sound out of the shofar. Finally, the rabbi himself took the shofar and brought it to his lips – but even he did not manage to make a sound. It was clear to all that the hand of Satan was involved.

Rabbi Levi Yitzhak put down the shofar that was in his hand and said: "Master of the universe! It is written in Your Torah, 'This day shall be for you a day when the horn is sounded' (Num. 29:1), since on this day You created the world. Look down from the heavens and see: we all assembled here with our whole families, our wives and our children, to perform Your will. But if it is denied us, and we are not Your beloved nation, then Ivan will blow the shofar!"

After a while, the rabbi took up the shofar again, and behold a clear, pure sound emerged.

After the prayers, the rabbi turned to his congregation and said, "We have prevailed. However, for this victory I have paid with my life, and now I am the atonement for Israel."

When Rabbi Levi Yitzhak left the synagogue at the end of Yom Kippur, he said to those with him, "You should know that today the days of my life have been completed, and it has been decreed that I must now leave the world. But I was very sad that I would not fulfill the two precious mitzvot which are coming in four days – the sukka and the etrog. So I prayed that I be given an extension."

And so it was. On the day after the Sukkot holiday, the rabbi of Berdichev became ill, and the next day he passed away.

The True King

It happened once that when Rabbi Levi Yitzhak reached the Kaddish prayer during the Rosh HaShana services, he said, "Punyah (a derogatory term for Russians, here directed at the czar) says that he is the king." He then listed the rest of the important kings, with their respective titles, and then he called out!

➳ ➳ ➳

The Advocate Versus the Prosecutor

Rabbi Yehuda Leib HaKohen Maimon (d. 1962) tells this story:

When Satan the Accuser would achieve the upper hand, and his prosecution of the People of Israel would intensify, and all hope was lost, Rabbi Levi Yitzhak of Berdichev would carry on his shoulders many bundles of merits. He would place them before the Throne of Glory, and say, "Here before You, our Father in heaven, are our deeds. Let them speak for themselves." And, as it were, God Himself would lift up the bundles and untie them; and when they were open, all the merits of the Jewish people rolled out, and surrounded the Throne of Glory, like white pigeons, and immediately Satan became confused and left, crushed.

But, during the days of *Seliḥot* one year, it seemed as if the gates of the heavens were closed to Rabbi Levi Yitzhak. He wrestled with the angel of Esau, and saw that he could not prevail. The hand of Satan was strong, and the tzaddik of Berdichev needed a great merit to prevail over the claims of Satan.

Rabbi Levi Yitzhak began to search for some special merit, and when he had finished reciting the *Seliḥot* prayers, he left the synagogue and secretly went to the dark passageways in the poor neighborhoods. He wandered through the alleys, searched and looked, and suddenly it seemed that there was a light shining on a lowly, crumbling house. He knew that here he would find what he was seeking.

He entered the house and noticed a young woman, head covered with a kerchief, sitting and reading *Teḥinot*. The woman recognized the tzaddik and was thoroughly shaken. She knew that it was the custom of Rabbi Levi Yitzhak during the days of *Seliḥot* to visit the houses of sinners, to persuade and rouse them to repent. And since he had come to her house, that meant that she must be a sinner. She broke out crying, "It is true that I sinned, my holy rabbi, but I have already repented, and have done all in my power to atone for my sin."

The tzaddik said to her, "Don't be sad, my daughter, you are not a sinner. You have great merit in heaven. But tell me please everything that happened to you."

This is the woman's story:

"My father and mother lived in a village not far from Berdichev, and made their living from a dairy farm which they leased from the owner of the village. When my dear parents died, I was seventeen years old. Since I was left an orphan, I went to the landlord to ask him not to remove me from my parents' holdings. As soon as the landlord saw me, he became filled with lust and began to speak to me in ugly language, and even tried to touch me with his filthy hands. I pushed him away and tried to flee, but then he changed his tone and began to speak to me gently: 'Heaven forbid that I do anything bad to you. I will give you a three-year lease on the dairy farm, and for half the price, just let me kiss the locks of your beautiful hair.' And as he talked, he grabbed my two long tresses of hair, caressed them, and kissed them lustfully.

"When I returned home, I could not rest. My heart thumped in guilt that I had allowed this evil man to contaminate me with his lips. All night long I did not sleep, I did not even close my eyes. In the morning, I took scissors and cut my hair, and the next day I left the village and the dairy farm and settled in the city. Here I was a servant for several years in the homes of wealthy people, until I was married. About a year ago my husband died, and I have pangs of conscience that he died because of my sin."

"And where are your shorn braids?" asked Rabbi Levi Yitzhak.

"Only one curl is left as a remembrance of my long braids," answered the woman, in pain, as she took out a curl from her pocket. "When my heart fills with sorrow about my bad luck, my oppression and travail, I take out this curl, stare at it and remember the sin of my youth, and accept my judgment."

A tear dropped from the eyes of Rabbi Levi Yitzhak, and he left her with his blessing.

Rosh HaShana arrived. Rabbi Levi Yitzhak sat until midnight, studying the talmudic Tractate Rosh HaShana. At dawn, he went to the *mikve* and dipped forty-two times, corresponding to the forty-two holy names in the prayer "*Ana beko'ah*," then he emerged and, dressed in his white garb, draped himself in his tallit and went to the beit midrash. The beit midrash was full of people, all covered with their tallitot, reciting the morning prayers. When they reached the prayer of "*HaMelekh*," all the worshipers fixed their gaze on their great rabbi, Rabbi Levi Yitzhak, as he draped the silver *atara* of his tallit over his head and face. After a minute, the rings and flourishes of sweet voices commingled and rolled along the walls of the beit midrash. The strong voice of the tzaddik was heard – "*HaMelekh*" – and he approached the pulpit and continued with the well-known melody filled with tenderness and sadness.

The large congregation responded and all the voices coalesced into one voice coming from one huge heart, and all the prayers mixed into one prayer, splitting the firmament. In the prayer "*Avinu Malkeinu*," the crying became stronger and arose to the heavens. From the prayers of the tzaddik, the worshipers sensed that the hand of the heretics had been strengthened and they stood as a barrier before the Throne of Glory. Who knows – they thought in their hearts – how many heaps upon heaps of accusations and slander have piled up there before the gates of heaven, to prevent the prayers of the Jewish people from rising and joining the crowns on the head of their Maker?

This thought pinched their souls as with white-hot pliers, and from the mouths of all the worshipers, and from the depth of their hearts, a wailing prayer broke out: "*Avinu Malkeinu*...annul from us all evil decrees.... Close the mouths of those who hate us and accuse us!"

Then the hour of the shofar blasts arrived. Everyone waited impatiently for their holy rabbi who had gone to immerse once more in the *mikve*. According to those closest to him, on that day he increased his devotions and meditations on God's oneness more than in any other year. From the multiple preparations of the tzaddik, everyone felt that there must be a strong accuser in heaven, and the People of Israel were in need of great mercy.

And then the tzaddik entered, dressed all in white, walking very slowly until he reached the pulpit where he stood erect, and again wrapped himself with his tallit over his face and his entire body, and lowered his head onto his arms, which were leaning on the rostrum. He stood silently, troubled groans emerging from his throat. Suddenly he raised his head, lifted his eyes to heaven, and began to plead:

"Master of the heavens, if our sins are heavy, if our faults weigh down the scales against us, I request from You and plea before You that You take the curl of hair of this forlorn woman and place it on the other side of the scale, and I am certain that this curl of hair will turn the scales in our favor."

Levi Yitzhak began to preach before his Maker in the presence of the entire congregation about this woman, who was orphaned while still a young woman, that she needed sustenance, and she went to the landowner to try to persuade him not to drive her off the land of her parents, and this son of Esau wanted to exploit her situation for his pleasure and his passion. This upright Jewish maiden refused, and the indecent landowner tried to seduce her by promising to rent her the dairy farm at half price, if only she will permit him to caress and kiss her hair. This poor orphan, who is exposed to hunger and need, could now change her situation for good – in exchange for one kiss – but she refused, this pure, innocent Hebrew soul, and the vile stranger used his power, the hand of Esau, and against her will he grabbed the braids of her hair and kissed them. And what did this daughter of Jacob do? She did not come with a grievance to the Blessed Holy One, who took away her parents and left her sighing. She blames herself, and as atonement for a sin she did not commit she cut her long braids, ran away from the village, went to work as a servant in the home of strangers for a morsel of bread – and found no rest, as it seems to her that she has a part in the sin of this foul evil man.

She was married to a man her age, and after a few years, he too passed away, again leaving her alone in life, poor and depressed, broken-hearted and exhausted. But she did not complain about the decree that afflicted her so harshly. She still blames herself, and, as a remembrance of her transgression, she peers from time to time at the curl of hair she cut off, and justifies the rightness of her judgment.

"Now I, Your servant, Levi Yitzhak, turn to You, just and merciful God, and I ask You: 'Does not this curl of hair demonstrate the great difference between a pure, upstanding daughter of Israel and the filthy, vile landowner? Does not this curl show clearly the special significance of those who declare Your unity with love – compared to the nations of the world, with their princes and vile landowners? And is not this curl of hair worthy to tip the scale of justice in favor of the People of Israel?'"

Immediately there was a clamor in the heavenly host, as the Blessed Omnipresent One came down, in all His honored glory, from His throne of justice and sat on the throne of mercy.

The claims of Samael were denied, the gates of heaven opened wide, the face of the tzaddik glowed from the joy and delight of victory, and that year was a year of blessing and success for the Jews.

⁊ ⁊ ⁊

The Crying Woman

Rabbi Levi Yitzhak told this story:

It happened once, shortly before Rosh HaShana, that a woman approached me crying bitterly. I asked her, "Why are you crying? Why are you crying?" She replied, "How can I not cry? My head hurts! My head hurts."

I said to her, "Do not cry! If you cry, your head will hurt even more."

She replied, "How can I not cry? I have only one son, and the holy day of awe is approaching, and I do not know if he will withstand the judgment of the Blessed Holy One."

I said to her, "Do not cry! He will surely pass the test, and be vindicated in judgment. Is it not written: Truly, Ephraim is a dear son to Me, a darling child! Whenever I have spoken of him, My thoughts would dwell on him still. That is why My heart yearns for him; I will receive him back in love – declares the Lord (Jer. 31:19)?"

Rabbi Levi Yitzhak related this story in a mystical tune, and with the same melody Hasidim tell this story until today.

Serving God

The Hasidic Method of Rabbi Levi Yitzhak

Rabbi Elimelekh of Lizhensk, author of *No'am Elimelekh*, taught:
The method of Rabbi Levi Yitzhak of Berdichev in hasidic teaching was much different than the method of Rabbi Shneur Zalman of Liadi, author of the *Tanya*. Rabbi Shneur Zalman based his method of Hasidism on three pillars: *Ḥokhma, Bina,* and *Daat* – hence the acronym *Ḥabad*.

Rabbi Levi Yitzhak of Berdichev had a different method. His method was built on the feeling of the heart, which burns with love and awe for the Creator of the world. Such burning love would bring spiritual elevation, without any theorizing or intellectual depth – "God desires the heart" (Sanhedrin 106b).

Tanya

When Rabbi Shneur Zalman of Liadi, the founder of the Chabad school of Hasidism, wrote the *Tanya*, the book was accepted by tzaddikim and Hasidim of his generation for its deep exploration into matters of divinity and methods of worshiping God.

When the book reached Rabbi Levi Yitzhak of Berdichev, he read it from cover to cover, and commented: "How wonderful are the deeds of Rabbi Shneur Zalman – he compressed a great and mighty God, the *Ein Sof*, into one small, thin book."

⋟⋟ ⋟⋟ ⋟⋟

On the Roof

It happened once that Rabbi Levi Yitzhak climbed up to the roof of his home, in the center of the marketplace, and cried out:

"Jews, seed of a holy people, remember and set upon your hearts, for what purpose are you racing, and to where are you racing?

"You remember everything, only the Blessed Creator do you forget."

⋟⋟ ⋟⋟ ⋟⋟

"Who Created All Things for Your Glory"

It happened once that Rabbi Levi Yitzhak of Berdichev poured out his sorrow and sadness to Rabbi Shneur Zalman of Liadi, that despite all his effort and labor, he did not merit to reach a level of worship of the Blessed One without the expectation of even a trace of honor.

"Levi Yitzhak my brother," replied Rabbi Shneur Zalman, "you can rest your mind. Come and see. About the Creator of the world, may His name be blessed, whom we are commanded to cling to and to walk in His ways, our sages said (Mishna Avot 6:12): All that the Blessed Holy One created in His world, He created solely for His glory, as it is written (Is. 43:7), 'All that is called by My name, indeed, it is for My glory that I have created it, formed it, and made it.'"

"Not so, my brother," replied Rabbi Levi Yitzhak. "There is no similar evidence here, since when it comes to God Himself, as it were, what He does for Himself is also for the sake of heaven."

Serving God

"The more one sanctifies and purifies himself,
And the more one serves God, may He be blessed,
The more he knows that he still has not begun to serve Him at all.
Because one who thinks that he is God's servant,
This is a sign that he is not serving God at all.
Because if he were serving Him,
He would know that he is very far from the Blessed God."

Shabbat

Saving a Life

It happened once that the tzaddik Rabbi Levi Yitzhak of Berdichev was traveling with two of his servants. On Friday, they reached a small town, and since it was the custom of the tzaddik not to travel on Fridays after noon he remained there for Shabbat.

As it happened, before the arrival of the tzaddik at that town, swindlers, disguised as tzaddikim, had come there on several occasions. They arrived with their servants, acted as though they were authentic tzaddikim, and managed to fool the public, until they were revealed as swindlers and scoundrels. When Rabbi Levi Yitzhak arrived, the townspeople assumed that he too was surely one of the swindlers. And to add to the confusion, one man said that he knew the rabbi of Berdichev and that this man did not resemble him at all. The people decided that the next day, on Shabbat, during the reading of the Torah, they would call him for an *aliya*, and disgrace and beat him.

The servants of the tzaddik realized that there was something amiss in the way the townspeople were looking at them, and they also believed they were conspiring against them. They therefore pleaded with the tzaddik to leave and go to another nearby town, which they could reach before Shabbat. But the tzaddik would not hear of it, insisting that never in his life had he traveled on Friday afternoon, and neither would he do so now.

Before sunset, the tzaddik went to the synagogue to greet Shabbat with the community. He recited the prayers, as usual, with an impassioned voice and enthusiastic motions. But the congregation, who had already decided that he was nothing but a swindler, stood in surprise, wondering, "How can this man blind the eyes of others, with these strange facial distortions that he makes?"

A gentile who was passing through the town at that hour on his way to a distant village heard the unusual sounds coming from the synagogue and asked a nearby Jew, "What are these sounds that we are hearing?"

The Jew answered, "Some visitor came here and says he is the rabbi of Berdichev, and he shouts thus when he prays."

The gentile continued on to the village and entered the tavern. After the customary greetings, the owner asked him about any news he had heard on his way. He replied, "I passed through a town and heard strange cries near the synagogue. So I asked for an explanation, and they told me that a certain rabbi was visiting and praying thus."

The owner asked, "And perhaps you know, who is the rabbi?"

"I think," replied the gentile, "that they told me that it was the rabbi of Berdichev."

Now, there was a teacher in the tavern who taught the children of the tavern owner, and this teacher knew the rabbi of Berdichev. He became very excited to hear that the tzaddik was in a nearby town – excited but also sorrowful. "Is it possible that the tzaddik is nearby, and I will not welcome him?" he said.

He could not calm down until he decided to go on foot, immediately, to the town to catch a glimpse of the tzaddik. And that is what he did. After he had walked a bit he stopped suddenly. A thought crossed his mind: "What am I doing? Is it not Shabbat today? From here to the town is too far to walk on Shabbat. Shall I continue walking and desecrate the Sabbath?"

The teacher stood deliberating until he decided: "So what! Since the tzaddik is here I must greet him."

He walked a bit further, and again stopped: "One may not perform a mitzva through a transgression. Is it permissible to violate the Sabbath in order to perform the mitzva of welcoming a rabbi?"

He stood and thought it over again, weighing all the aspects, and decided, "I must go!"

Again he walked a bit and stopped, and thus he did all night – walked a bit, regretted it, and walked some more, until, by morning, he found himself standing near the town.

When he reached it, the congregation was already standing in prayer in the synagogue. When he entered, they were reading the Torah, and the tzaddik had just ascended the pulpit. The townspeople had already prepared themselves to "honor" the swindler, when the door opened and the teacher, who was known in the town as a learned and pious man, burst into the synagogue. When he saw the tzaddik standing on the pulpit, he ran toward him, frightened, and yelled in a loud wail, "Rabbi, oy, I desecrated the Sabbath!"

The tzaddik said to him, "You did not desecrate the Sabbath, because your coming here saved my life. Had you not come I would have been in great danger."

Then the congregants realized that this man was truly the rabbi of Berdichev, and asked his forgiveness for their unjustified suspicion.

The Clothing That Remained Unwashed

"I can no longer hold back," said Rabbi Levi Yitzhak of Berdichev to his servant. "I must spend a Shabbat with Rabbi Barukh of Mezhibush (d. 1811), grandson of the holy Baal Shem Tov." The servant peered at his rabbi in surprise. It was not a secret among the Hasidim that their rabbi had, for a long time, wanted to spend Shabbat with Rabbi Barukh but was prevented from doing so because of the great differences in their personal behavior. While Rabbi Barukh was a very orderly man, fastidious with his clothing and austere in behavior, Rabbi Levi Yitzhak was inclined to be full of enthusiasm and joy, and did not pay much attention to his garments, and so on.

Rabbi Levi Yitzhak knew that it would be very difficult for him to scrupulously comply with the whole behavioral regimen in Rabbi Barukh's home. Therefore he had avoided visiting him for Shabbat. However, he could no longer restrain his desire, so he decided that he was prepared to observe all the rules of polite behavior and orderliness in exchange for an invitation to spend Shabbat with Rabbi Barukh.

On Friday evening, no sooner had the cantor begun the evening service with *Lekhu Neranena*, than Rabbi Levi Yitzhak felt an intense need to call out *"Shabbat kodesh!"*, but, faithful to his promise, he remained silent. At the chanting of *Lekha Dodi* he restrained himself with difficulty, and did not break out in wild dancing. The same with *Shalom Aleikhem*.

When Rabbi Barukh began to chant the Kiddush, Rabbi Levi Yitzhak could barely contain himself. He bit his lower lip trying to stifle the *niggun* which nearly erupted loudly. Rabbi Levi Yitzhak's heart was filled with enormous joy that he merited to observe Shabbat with the wonderful tzaddik, the grandson of the Baal Shem Tov. After a short while, one of the Hasidim approached the important guest, carrying a large tray piled high with all kinds of meat dishes. "May I offer the honored rabbi a portion of meat in honor of Shabbat?" asked the Hasid. "We have a large variety. Does the rabbi prefer chicken or shnitzel?" Rabbi Levi Yitzhak became so excited that he forgot his promise, and blurted out, "I, I love only God!" And in his extreme enthusiasm he knocked the tray out of the hand of the Hasid and pushed it toward the ceiling. Naturally, the clothes of those present were soiled, including the clothes of Rabbi Barukh.

When Rabbi Barukh saw the tremendous love of God burning in the heart of Rabbi Levi Yitzhak, he decided that he would preserve those clothes with the dirt on them and never wash them.

Sin and Transgression

Tefillin of *Teshuva*

There was a custom in Berdichev whereby the *gabbai* of the *ḥevra kaddisha* would take the tefillin of the deceased people and sell them for the benefit of the *ḥevra*.

It happened once that the tzaddik Rabbi Levi Yitzhak came to the *gabbai* and requested that he show him all the pairs of tefillin in his possession, since he wanted to select one set for himself. The *gabbai* showed him all the sets, and the tzaddik selected one, and told the *gabbai* that this was the pair he wanted to buy.

The *gabbai* realized that the tzaddik would not go to the *ḥevra kaddisha* to buy ready-made tefillin, so there must be some special reason. Therefore, he said to the tzaddik:

"Rabbi! All the sets of tefillin found here are available, except this pair. This pair is not for sale."

The tzaddik pressed him to sell this pair. Finally, the *gabbai* said to him: "I will agree to sell you this pair of tefillin on condition that you tell me what is so special about them, that you want them so badly."

The tzaddik answered: "The holy brothers, Rabbi Elimelekh and Rabbi Zusha, were accustomed to wander through villages and towns, to bring sinners back to Judaism. This is how they did it. When they came to an inn to stay, one of them would turn to the other, as a sinner would turn to his rabbi, and he would relate, with tears in his eyes, all his 'sins,' and request that the rabbi would permit him to do *teshuva*. He would list all the sins that the innkeeper had committed, but would accuse himself of doing them. The innkeeper, hearing these things, would recall that he too had committed the same sins, and would do *teshuva*.

"On one occasion, they visited a village and, as was their custom, stayed at the home of a Jew who lived in the village. During the evening, Rabbi Zusha began to cry and asked his brother to let him do *teshuva*, since his whole life he had never inspected his pair of tefillin, and now that he had inspected them he had discovered that they were empty – missing all four biblical passages. So, it turned out that during his whole life he was what the rabbis called 'a head with no tefillin.' Rabbi Elimelekh began to reprove him about this matter, even exaggerating the sin.

"The host was listening to this whole conversation, and suddenly an idea flashed in his head: 'I too have never inspected my tefillin!' Immediately, he ran in haste, grabbed his tefillin, opened them, and lo and behold, they were completely empty, missing all four biblical passages!

"The man panicked, approached the holy brothers, and confessed to them the terrible failure that happened also to him, regarding his tefillin. He cried and begged them to arrange *teshuva* for him.

"Rabbi Elimelekh said to Rabbi Zusha, 'Right away inscribe the four passages on parchment for this man, with the intention of bringing light to a person who never wore tefillin his whole life.'

"Rabbi Zusha inscribed the biblical passages, placed them inside the tefillin boxes, and gave them to the man. However, the light and the holiness of these tefillin were overpowering, beyond the ability of this man to tolerate. Not long after, the man died in Berdichev.

"These are the tefillin," concluded the tzaddik of Berdichev, "which ended up in the custody of the *ḥevra kaddisha*."

ﻉ ﻉ ﻉ

"Woe unto the Father Who Exiled His Children"

It happened once that a devout Jewish preacher, a *maggid*, who traveled through the cities collecting donations as he went, came to Berdichev. He visited Rabbi Levi Yitzhak, the chief rabbi, to ask permission to preach in the beit midrash.

Rabbi Levi Yitzhak replied, "Permission is granted, as long as you speak words of Torah, and not about sins, transgressions, and crimes." The *maggid* agreed to the condition. Rabbi Levi Yitzhak even came to the beit midrash in order to increase the prestige of the *maggid*, enlarge the number of attendees, and enhance his earnings.

The *maggid* began discussing the Torah portion of the week, and gave several interpretations. Since he skipped around and jumped from one subject to another, he did not restrain his inclination and began discussing the subject of Jewish law. He chided the Jews for their lack of Torah study and their absence of generosity in *tzedaka*, and criticized those who were guilty of gossip and slander. In this fashion, he continued to list the sins of the community.

Immediately Rabbi Levi Yitzhak rose, lifted his eyes heavenward, and said: "Master of the universe, please, in Your great mercy, pay no attention to the words of this speaker, and do not believe him. By my life, I swear that Your people Israel are all beloved, all pure, all righteous, and all holy. This poor man's troubles are speaking for him. His children are beset by hunger, his daughters have reached maturity and he does not have funds to marry them off. He is bitter and resentful. Please, God, You who provide and sustain everyone, endow him with sustenance enough to feed his family and make weddings for his daughters, so that he will no longer accuse Your holy people Israel."

Rabbi Levi Yitzhak spoke further to the *maggid*: "My dear brother, did you say all these things to fulfill your obligations to God? Now that you have chastised the Jewish people for their sins against their Father in heaven, it is only fair and decent that you demand justice from your Maker. Tell Him, 'Your unfortunate children have been expelled from their Father's table, and they are saddened, slaughtered, burned, and dying as martyrs for Your sacred name. Woe unto the Father who exiled His children.'"

A Parable of a Garment

Rabbi Levi Yitzhak was asked: "May our rabbi teach us, what should a person do if in his heart was aroused a strong love for something vain, and it distracts him, and he cannot rid himself of it, even though he is sorry about it and recognizes its worthlessness?"

Rabbi Levi Yitzhak replied: "The matter is thus. Sometimes the person cannot drive out an inappropriate attraction from his heart in any way. My advice is not to chase it away, or run away from it, lest, God forbid, it chase after him. Rather, he should try to pay attention to it and raise it to a higher level.

"In other words, he should examine that which arouses his love and clarify its source, what is the power that sustains it, and whence comes its particular charm. At that moment, he will understand that the charm is the vitality in it, and the vitality is the spark that emanates from the flame of life.

"And who lit the flame of life? Is it not our Blessed Creator?

"After he makes this reckoning for himself, the person will clearly say to himself: 'Whyever am I attracted to this? It is only a mere spark of the great flame. Would it not be better for me to be connected by the strength of the love aroused in me to the First Cause, to the Blessed Creator, who sustains all living things?'

"When he considers these things, a feeling of love for the Source of life will be strengthened, and he will see that not only has his love for this worldly object not been chased away with humiliation, but that he has raised the love itself to a higher level; and because he has drawn to his lowly love the bounty of the Almighty, and used it to come closer to the Creator, he has redeemed the emotion of love itself from its corruption and raised it in holiness. In other words, he banished the evil and the defect in that love and replaced it with pure goodness.

"What is this compared to? To a garment which was sullied by thorns and dirt and dust that you shake out to get rid of the dirt and dust."

≫ ≫ ≫

How Much More So

Rabbi Levi Yitzhak of Berdichev traveled throughout the area to collect charity for the redemption of captives. He tarried, going from city to city, yet he did not succeed in collecting the full amount. The tzaddik paused to reflect, and said to himself, "Perhaps I did not act properly. I neglected my Torah study and my regular prayers, and came up with nothing. Better I should have sat in my house and studied and prayed."

It happened that in the town where Rabbi Levi Yitzhak was staying at the time, a Jew was caught stealing. He was beaten and locked up in jail.

"Look here, my son," said Rabbi Levi Yitzhak to the thief. "See what you did to yourself. Remember this and do not go back to your evil ways."

"So what?" answered the thief. "If I did not succeed today, I will succeed tomorrow."

At that moment, Rabbi Levi Yitzhak drew a comparison to himself: "If this simple fellow does not despair despite the punishment for his transgression, how much more so that I not cease from the mitzva of collecting *tzedaka*. If I did not succeed today, I will succeed tomorrow, or the day after."

Outwitting the Hasid

Lately, the *yetzer hara* has turned clever. Why should he struggle and wrestle with the quick-wittedness of the sharpest Hasidim?

So he secretly comes and offers a suggestion to fast often.

Then the Hasid will fast frequently until his mind weakens, and his senses become disoriented.

Only then is the *yetzer hara* sure to win out.

Soul and Spirit

"The Soul You Gave Me"

When Rabbi Levi Yitzhak of Berdichev went to the funeral of his son, he did not shed a tear.

When he was asked why, he answered, "A pure soul was given to me, and I am returning a pure soul."

The Sanctuary of the *Niggun*

Once, on a summer day, Rabbi Levi Yitzhak of Berdichev recited the morning prayers early in the morning, to the great surprise of his friends, since he was not accustomed to pray so early. After the prayers, he ordered a wagon driver to take him to a village about thirty parasangs (120 miles) from the city.

Several of the rabbi's friends went with him. They traveled all day, and toward evening they came to a village and the home of the estate manager of the village leader. They asked if they could stay overnight. This man was an evil person, a Jew who had distanced himself from his people and his religion, a glutton and a drunkard. When they pressed him repeatedly, he agreed, and Rabbi Levi Yitzhak prepared to recite his prayers.

Before Rabbi Levi Yitzhak could begin even the first words of the evening prayer – "May the merciful God forgive sins" – he sank into deep devotion, and chanted a *niggun* in sadness and supplication from the bottom of his heart, as one who is seeking mercy for his soul. Then he began to chant another part of the *niggun*, a strain of joy and enthusiasm with deep yearning. Finally he began to chant, "May the merciful ...," and finished the sentence with a *niggun* of joy and enthusiasm.

Word spread quickly all around the village that the tzaddik Rabbi Levi Yitzhak had arrived and was reciting his prayers. Some thirty people gathered from the village and from nearby villages to welcome the tzaddik and to hear his songs and his prayers. They all became so excited from Rabbi Levi Yitzhak's heart-piercing *niggun* that they stood in amazement, not recognizing their neighbors or themselves, and melted from deep joy and benevolence.

They all peered into the depth of their souls, and took an account of themselves. Engrossed in their inner selves, it seemed they didn't see or hear anything. Only the book of memories of their past lives was open before them.

With every part of the *niggun* from the mouth of Rabbi Levi Yitzhak, the listeners sank into the bitterness of their souls and absorbed the shame of their past deeds. The notes sounded the intense longing of the soul to the point of exhaustion. Their souls cried over their bodies, their bodies mourned for their souls, and both together melted in bitterness. Indeed, the souls and the bodies clung to each other, both yearning for life, but feeling that their minutes were numbered – another minute, another second, and their separation would be near.

Suddenly, a loud sound was heard, a sound announcing good news: Rabbi Levi Yitzhak began chanting the same *niggun*

with joy and gladness. His voice was strong, carrying outpour-
ings of hope, redemption, and salvation, a bonding of soul, faith,
and confidence. A new vitality penetrated their souls, uplifting
the spirit. The *niggun* touched them in the deepest places of their
hearts. Everyone standing there was touched and uplifted, but
only his friends understood the essence of the *niggun*. Rabbi Levi
Yitzhak described with the *niggun* the matter of the descent of the
soul into the body. It was not only a *niggun*, but also a story.

It was the story of souls hovering in a world which is entirely
radiance, purity, and spiritual delight, whose time arrives to
descend to the lower world and be clothed in a body. The beginning of the *niggun* describes the soul's feeling at the moment it discovers that it must descend into the body. Immediately, it begins
to leave its place in the treasure store of souls, and the parting is
difficult. It leaves the supernal lights. It departs from its friends,
the other souls, and from the angel who teaches them Torah.

After the soul receives blessings of farewell from all of them,
it goes on its mission to the material world, and in that moment
terrible bitterness seizes it because it does not know where it will
be led. As long as the souls are found among the others in the
treasure store of souls, they have no awareness of the nature of
this world and no concept of a physical body. Thus, on its way to
this world, the soul is tormented.

It is vital to know this: souls are not angels. Angels know that
there is a lower world and they know its nature, that it has good and
evil, the good inclination and the evil inclination. Angels are also
informed about the events in this world from new angels, which
are created in this world by the mitzvot that people do. Souls, on
the other hand, know nothing about the affairs of this world. There
are some, though, who have some idea of such affairs, and they
are the ones who were encased in bodies, and went up to heaven,
and then were ordered to return and be clothed in physical bodies.

The procedure of a soul's descent into a body is thus: on its way from the treasure store of souls, it is taken to *Gan Eden*, where it is told about the nature of this world.

And when the soul enters *Gan Eden*, it sees the tzaddikim sitting in sanctuaries, such as the holy forefathers, the *Tanna'im* and *Amora'im*, the tzaddikim and their pupils of all the generations. The soul is taken from *Gan Eden* and positioned near *Gehinom* so it can see the punishments of the wicked. It is then told that the choice between *Gan Eden* and *Gehinom* can be made only by the person who is capable of choosing. It is easy for us to imagine the pain of the soul as it descends from the upper world, since it has already learned what the nature of the lower world is – the world of falsehood.

This world is known as the world of falsehood since the entire reality in this world is based on vanity and falsehood. Materialism is falsehood. The true reality is only in spiritual existence. The materialistic reality overshadows the spiritual one. People speak lies, and no one knows what is in the heart of his neighbor. Everyone carries in his heart his own secrets, flaws, blemishes, known only to him, which he takes great pains to hide from others.

The journey from the world of truth to the world of falsehood greatly depresses the soul. Then, when it enters this world, it falls into the hands of the *yetzer hara*, which plots all kinds of tricks to distract it from the spiritual experience, and imbeds it into the midst of contemptible materialism.

The beginning of the *niggun*, sung by Rabbi Levi Yitzhak before the prayer "May the merciful God forgive sins," was like a dirge sung by the soul in its travels from the realm of purity in the treasure store of souls to the gloomy valley of this materialistic world. But the second part of the *niggun* sounded like a harbinger of joy and gladness, which is found in the last verse of the prayer,

"Lord, redeem us! Our Sovereign, answer us when we call." This part of the *niggun* proclaims the great kindness of the Blessed Creator, which descends on all who want to be servants of God.

Now, since the character of the *niggun* has become clear, the words of the prayer "May the merciful God forgive sins...Lord, redeem us!" have also been elucidated.

Immediately, at the start of the prayers with the sound of the *niggun*, the spirit of the evil Jew, who was alienated from his people and religion, was broken. And when Rabbi Levi Yitzhak concluded the prayer with a joyous and happy voice, and with great enthusiasm, this evil man fell to the ground with arms and legs extended, and cried in repentance, prayer, and regret.

This is the meaning of the *niggun*, which was a story.

From this, Rabbi Levi Yitzhak's friends understood why he visited this village, and why he rushed to recite the morning prayers so early, in contrast to his normal custom.

Spirituality and Materiality

True Love

"There are some who love their wives with a physical desire,
And so fulfill their desire.
It turns out that such men do not love their wives at all;
Rather they love only themselves."

Such Is the Reward for Observing Torah?

It happened once that Rabbi Levi Yitzhak of Berdichev heard a Jew pouring out his heart to a *maggid*, complaining to him about his terrible situation, that things are very bad, that endless troubles surround him, and all this at a time when he is trying with all his might to go in the right path, and to worship God. He never hurt anyone, heaven forbid, and he cannot understand why he deserves to suffer so much. "Is it possible," sighed the Jew, "that this is the reward for observing the Torah? And that in this world one does not deserve any reward, not even a scrap of bread?"

The *maggid* tried to comfort him, and explained to him that it is true that a small part of the reward for good deeds is allotted in this world. But that reward is not in unimportant material things, but rather in spiritual matters, in spiritual pleasures.

"Don't believe him, Reb Jew," said Rabbi Levi Yitzhak, turning toward him. "It's not true. The troubles that the Master of the universe rains on you are not spiritual troubles – they are real troubles, material troubles. Therefore, He is obligated to give you material rewards. Your complaints, dear Jew, are all true and just!"

"And You Shall Eat, and Be Satisfied, and Bless"

At the wedding of the grandchildren of Rabbi Levi Yitzhak of Berdichev and Rabbi Shneur Zalman of Liadi, Shneur Zalman lifted a glass to make a toast of "*LeHayim*" in honor of Rabbi Levi Yitzhak, and said, "*LeHayim*, my dear in-law," and he blessed him, "May we be blessed both in material and in spiritual matters."

Rabbi Levi Yitzhak asked him, "First material blessings, and only then spiritual blessings?"

Rabbi Shneur Zalman replied, "Even our father Jacob put material things before spiritual things – 'If God gives me bread to eat and clothing to wear…the Lord shall be my God' (Gen. 28:20–21)."

Rabbi Levi Yitzhak asked, "Is it possible to compare the material blessings of Jacob to those of ours?"

Rabbi Shneur Zalman answered, "Is it possible that the spiritual blessings of Jacob are similar to ours?"

Sukkot

In the Future

"At some future time, all the tzaddikim will be invited to enter the
'sukka made with the skin of Leviathan.'
But I, Levi Yitzhak, I also will desire
To enter that same sukka.
Surely the angel at the entrance will prevent me from entering
and ask me angrily:
'Hey – How do you deserve this, a simple fellow like you,
To push yourself in here among the tzaddikim and giants of
the world?'
I will reply: 'Do not be angry.
To me, to my sukka,
I permitted simple people to enter,
And I was not at all embarrassed by them.'"

He Did Not Feel the Pain

During the festival of Sukkot, when Rabbi Levi Yitzhak wanted
to put his hand into the cabinet in which the etrog and lulav were

stored, in order to make the blessing "*Al netilat lulav*," he put his hand through the glass cover, and did not even feel that he had cut himself.

"*SheHeḥeyanu*"

It was the custom of Rabbi Levi Yitzhak to arise before dawn on the first day of the Festival of Sukkot. He would enter his sukka and wait with intense longing for sunrise, so he could recite the blessing on the Four Species.

At the same time, some of his Hasidim, as well as many others, would gather in his sukka in order to recite the traditional blessing with him.

With sunrise, Rabbi Levi Yitzhak would jump with joy, take the Four Species, and with great excitement recite "*Al netilat lulav*" and "*SheHeḥeyanu*." With hasidic passion he began to dance, one hand holding the Four Species and the other hand pulling each and every one into the dancing circle.

Once, one of the *dayanim* of Berdichev came to Rabbi Levi Yitzhak's sukka on this occasion. The gentleman did not approve of Hasidim, and when he saw the dancing, a slight grin appeared on his face. One of the Hasidim noticed this and began to sing, in a hasidic tune, the biblical phrase "You shall rejoice in your festival." Rabbi Levi Yitzhak understood that this Hasid was directing his chant at the *dayan* who was sneering at the dancing, and the rabbi turned to the Hasid and told him in a loud voice:

"You fool! Even if it were not written in the Torah 'Rejoice in your festival,' would Levi Yitzhak not be full of joy that he was privileged to dwell in the sukka and bless the Four Species as he was commanded by the Blessed Holy One?"

"Pri Etz Hadar"

It happened that in a certain year there was a great shortage of etrogim and, with difficulty, a single etrog was acquired for all the community of Berdichev. Naturally, this etrog was kept by the tzaddik Rabbi Levi Yitzhak, and everyone in the city had to go to the home of the tzaddik to recite the blessing.

The tzaddik had one regular servant. The servant thought to himself that immediately after the tzaddik made the blessing, surely next in line to bless the etrog would be the Hasidim and leaders, and after them the wealthy people, the philanthropists, and the other important people in the city – so until his own turn came, it would be evening. Then the *yetzer hara* began to gnaw at him: "Why should my portion be diminished? Am I not a Jew like them? And since I merited to serve the tzaddik I should lose out?"

The servant did not calm down until he decided that early in the morning, while the tzaddik was still busy immersing in the *mikve* and reciting special prayers, he would secretly take the etrog and recite the blessing over it. And so he did.

When dawn broke on the first day of the festival, and the tzaddik was bathing in the *mikve*, the servant quietly took the etrog, hoping to recite the blessing over it. But as the devil would have it, a terrible accident occurred. Because of his fright and apprehension lest someone become aware of what he was doing, the servant's hands trembled, the etrog fell on the ground, and the stem broke off. The etrog was no longer kosher for use!

The servant almost fainted from anguish. What to do? What to do? Not only would it be a disgrace when word got out that he had tried to recite the blessing over the etrog before the tzaddik, but also he had rendered the etrog completely not kosher for use. Rabbi Levi Yitzhak would be left without an etrog! And he, the servant, will have been responsible for it! There was nothing he could do. He would have to report the matter to the tzaddik, just as it happened, and whatever would be, would be.

The servant sat distressed and worried about the terrible tragedy until the tzaddik came to recite the blessing over the etrog. Weeping bitterly, the servant explained what had happened. He assumed that surely the tzaddik would be furious over this event that should never have happened.

How amazed was the servant to see that the tzaddik was not irate or angry at all. Rather, he took the etrog in his two hands and with great enthusiasm, as was his wont, began to sing the servant's praises before the Blessed Holy One:

"Master of the universe! Please take notice how beloved are the mitzvot to the Jewish people, such that a simple Jew like my servant, in his zeal to fulfill the mitzva of blessing the etrog, put himself in jeopardy of ruining the etrog just so he could be counted among those who hasten to perform mitzvot."

Teshuva of Love

It happened once on the morning of the first day of Sukkot that Rabbi Levi Yitzhak of Berdichev hurried into the beit midrash and announced in a loud voice: "Who of you, fellow Jews, has committed a transgression? From every corner of your hearts, search and bring me your transgressions. As explicated in the Midrash on the biblical verse, 'You shall take for yourselves on the first day – the first day of counting transgressions.' On Rosh HaShana and on Yom Kippur a Jew does *teshuva* out of fear, and at that moment his willful sins are counted as mistakes. And on Sukkot, when a Jew fulfills and honors the mitzva of the Four

Species, he does *teshuva* out of love. At that moment, his willful sins are counted as merits. Therefore, the more old transgressions, which remained hidden in the corners of the heart, the more merits it is possible to acquire with them. Remember, therefore, dear Jews, whoever has any transgression should hurry and add it to the balance."

Teshuva

There Is Nothing So Whole as a Broken Heart

"A person who does *teshuva* out of fear,
And how much more so out of love,
And rends his heart into thousands of pieces,
The Blessed Holy One has mercy and gives the person a healthy
    and whole heart,
Strong and sturdy to worship the Blessed One.
From here we can conclude:
There is nothing in the world so repaired and whole
As a broken heart."

Sins That Become Merits

It happened once that, in his travels, Rabbi Levi Yitzhak of Berdichev met a man, a notorious, lawless glutton, an apostate, who
did not accept anything in the Torah. Rabbi Levi Yitzhak began
to speak kindly to him: "My dear brother, how I envy you! You
yourself have no idea what an inestimable treasure you carry with

you. Our sages taught, 'One who repents out of love, his evil deeds are counted as merits' (Yoma 86b).

"Therefore, if you were to just open your heart and overcome, and decide to return in repentance, all your sins that you committed in your entire life would be considered as merits. No tzaddik would be equal to you, since no one would be blessed with so many merits."

These heartfelt words moved the apostate so deeply that he immediately returned in repentance, and became a well-known and respected Hasid.

Exchange

It happened once that in the middle of his prayers to the Blessed Creator, Rabbi Levi Yitzhak said: "Master of the universe, a long time ago You offered Your Torah to all the nations, as a merchant who offers spoiled apples, and they refused to accept it from You. They did not even want to glance at You. But we, the People of Israel, accepted it.

"Therefore I want to make a trade with You. We have a large pile of sins, transgressions, and crimes, and You have an abundance of pardon, forgiveness, and atonement. Therefore, let us make an exchange. But lest You think, is this a fair trade? No! Had we not sins, what would You do with Your forgiveness? Therefore, You are obligated to add for us life, children, and sustenance."

Each and Every Day

Every night Rabbi Levi Yitzhak would examine his actions of the day, and repent for every mistake he had made, and say, "Levi Yitzhak will not do that again."

Immediately he would say to himself, "Levi Yitzhak, you said the same thing last night." Then he said to himself, "Last night Levi Yitzhak did not tell the truth, but today he is telling the truth."

He would say, "Like a woman giving birth, suffering birth pangs, who swears that she will no longer oblige her husband, and later forgets her oath, so do we confess our sins on Yom Kippur and we repent, but afterward we continue to sin, and You continue to forgive us!"

Perennial Beginnings

A certain student asked his rabbi, the tzaddik of Berdichev, "In the Talmud it is written: 'In a place where *baalei teshuva* stand, complete tzaddikim cannot stand' (Berakhot 34b). Does this mean that whoever has done no misdeeds from the time of his youth is not as pious as one who has many transgressions and sins to God, and cannot reach his level?"

"Whoever discovers every day," answered the tzaddik, "new lights that the day before he did not know, if he wants to worship in truth, must negate his faulty worship of the day before and repent and start from the beginning. And the one who has no faults, and who imagines that his worship is perfected and complete and he is constant with it, does not capture the light, and he lags behind the one who is always doing repentance."

Something to Repair

On Rosh Ḥodesh Elul, the tzaddik Rabbi Levi Yitzhak of Berdichev stood at the window of his study, looking out at the marketplace. It was early in the morning and the market square was almost empty. Suddenly, a deep-voiced male advertised his handiwork in a monotone to a handful of passersby. Immediately, the man himself appeared, approaching in measured and rapid steps. It was Ivan the shoemaker, carrying on his back a haphazard pile of tools in a worn satchel, from which stuck out several faded leather straps.

When Ivan passed by the window of Rabbi Levi Yitzhak, he noticed the figure looking out of the window and called out in a loud voice, "Rabbi! Do you not have something to repair?"

Rabbi Levi Yitzhak was frightened by the voice of Ivan the shoemaker. And when the shoemaker was gone, the tzaddik sat down on the ground, covered his face with his hands, and with bitter tears said, "This gentile is asking me if I don't have something to fix. Here it is Rosh Ḥodesh Elul today, and surely I have many things to fix. Woe is me, how many important things I have to fix in the month of mercy and forgiveness!"

This World and the Next World

A Clear Sign

"The world is a hospitable place.
And here is a clear sign:
It tolerates someone like me."

There Is No Substitute

On the twenty-fifth day of the month of Tishrei, 1809, the upper world conquered the lower world, and the soul of Rabbi Levi Yitzhak of Berdichev returned to the source of its being. He had become ill immediately after Yom Kippur and was near death, but he prayed that he be granted several more days in order to be able to recite the blessing over the Four Species. His prayer was accepted, and he lived until the day after Sukkot.

Thousands followed his casket. The tzaddikim of the generation eulogized him at length and said that a deep darkness had covered them with the departure of this tzaddik, who excelled in piety. However, in the upper world there was joy, happiness, and a great light, since an exceptional soul had ascended there to dwell in *Gan Eden*. And thus they interpreted the biblical verse in *Kohelet* (Eccl. 3:4), "A time for wailing and a time for dancing," to mean that at the same time, when the great tzaddik passed away, "wailing and dancing" joined together – since in the lower world there was wailing and in the upper world there was dancing.

The citizens of Berdichev refused to be comforted upon the death of their rabbi. They decided that from then on there would not be a rabbi in their city, but only a *dayan* and righteous teacher, since no one was fit to fill the shoes of Rabbi Levi Yitzhak.

Repair

When Rabbi Levi Yitzhak was appointed rabbi of Berdichev, the *Mitnagdim* opposed him because he was a follower of Hasidism. Among them were a group who cherished the memory of Rabbi Eliezer Lieber (d. 1771), who lived in Berdichev the previous fifteen years, and taught Torah there. They refused to have any contact with the newcomer.

It happened once that Rabbi Levi Yitzhak called this group to him, and he told them that he planned to immerse himself in the *mikve* of Rabbi Lieber. However, Rabbi Lieber did not have a conventional *mikve*, but rather a type of roof leaning on four pillars, under which was a basin of water. In the winter, Rabbi Lieber would take a hatchet and break the ice, then immerse himself in the water. After his death, the roof collapsed and the basin was filled with mud. The tzaddik was informed that it was impossible to immerse there. However, the tzaddik stood his ground and hired four workers who dug there for an entire day. The next day the basin was again filled with mud. The same thing happened on the next few days. His opponents mocked the new rabbi, whom they saw as strange in his ways. "Everyone sees and senses," they said to him, "that Rabbi Lieber does not permit others to immerse in his *mikve*."

Rabbi Levi Yitzhak ordered all his loyal followers who still remembered Rabbi Lieber to gather early the next morning. The tzaddik accompanied them to the place where the workers were digging. After some two hours, one of them called out, "Behold, we see water." Quickly they informed the rabbi that some water had collected. "There is no need to dig any more," said the rabbi. He immediately took his clothes off and descended into the *mikve*. When he went into the water, it reached only to his ankles, but in an instant, the waters rose to his mouth.

Then he asked, "Is there anyone who still remembers Rabbi Lieber when he was in his youth?" Someone replied that in the new section of the city there still lived a servant, now an old man of one hundred years, who served Rabbi Lieber when he was young. The tzaddik ordered to summon him, and he waited in the water, which reached his mouth. At first, the old man refused to come, but when they related to him the whole story he came, along with the messenger.

"Do you still remember," asked the rabbi, "the synagogue attendant who hanged himself in the synagogue on the large candelabrum that was suspended from the ceiling?"

"I remember him," replied the man in surprise. "But what connection is there between him and you? Seventy years have already passed since then, and you were not even born yet!"

"Tell the story just as it happened!" said the rabbi.

The old man told this story: "He was a simple fellow, but very pious. He had a unique custom. Every Wednesday, in honor of Shabbat, he would begin to shine the candelabrum hanging on the ceiling, and while doing it he would say, 'I am doing this in

honor of the Blessed One.' Once when people came to the synagogue on Friday afternoon, they found him hanging by his belt
on the large candelabrum."

The rabbi said: "Since it was Shabbat eve, and everything was
clean and shining, and there was nothing more to do, the synagogue
attendant asked himself, 'What else can I do to honor the Creator?'
Immediately his mind became confused and perplexed, and since
the candelabrum hanging on the ceiling was in his eyes the biggest
thing in the world, he hanged himself on it, to honor the Blessed
One. And since it is now already seventy years later, Rabbi Lieber
appeared to me in a dream and requested that I do whatever I can
to redeem this pathetic soul. That is why I gave an order to repair
the holy *mikve* and I immersed in its waters. Now tell me please,
has the time come for the redemption of this pathetic soul?"

"Yes, yes, yes," cried the entire community with one voice.
"I agree, yes, yes, yes," said the rabbi, "Go in peace!" He then came
up out of the water, and immediately the water receded so that it
reached only to the soles of his feet.

Rabbi Levi Yitzhak ordered to have a bath house built on
that spot, to again repair the *mikve*, and to build a different *mikve*
for him. And only when the need arose, when some major event
was to take place, would he bathe in the *mikve* of Rabbi Lieber.

To this day, there stands in the old city, next to the beit
midrash, a bath house in which there are two *mikvaot* – one is
called the "*Mikve* of Rabbi Lieber," and the other, the "*Mikve* of
Rabbi Levi Yitzhak."

One Minute of Sadness

It was Rabbi Levi Yitzhak's custom to inquire about all the sick
people in the city, and to visit them. It happened once that he

visited a certain ill individual, and found him in anguish. Rabbi Levi Yitzhak asked him why he was worried.

The ill person replied, "Rabbi, I am afraid that my time is limited, and my heart is full of fear for what will be my lot in the next world."

Rabbi Levi Yitzhak said to him, "I am presenting to you as a free gift my entire portion in the next world." Immediately, they concluded the transaction. The sick man became very happy, but within an hour, he died.

One of Rabbi Levi Yitzhak's friends said to him, "Rabbi, surely your intention was to keep the sick man alive for a little while. But you saw that it was the final hour of this dying man, and that your encouragement would not help at all. What, therefore, was the need for all this?"

"Listen, my son," replied Rabbi Levi Yitzhak. "I would be content to give up my share in the World to Come in order to spare a mortally ill Jew one minute of sadness."

Bringing Merit to Many

This story was told by Rabbi Samuel Dresner:

Even though it is permissible to fulfill the mitzva of *brit mila* at any hour of the day, Rabbi Levi Yitzhak was accustomed to arise early in the morning to fulfill this mitzva before recitation of the morning prayers. However, only on one occasion did he fulfill the mitzva of *brit mila* later – at four o'clock in the afternoon! This is what happened.

A son was born to Rabbi Levi Yitzhak's daughter. All the important citizens of the city, as well as all his friends who lived outside the city, were invited for the *brit mila* of the newborn. Everyone gathered, from near and far, Hasidim and people of substance. On the eighth day after the child's birth, everyone rose early and went to the beit midrash, since they knew that the rabbi was strict about bringing the child into the covenant of our father Abraham early in the morning. When the sun rose, the rabbi's beit midrash could barely contain all those assembled. The hour of reciting Shaḥarit, the morning prayers, arrived and the crowd sat and waited for the rabbi, but he remained in his room.

An hour passed, then another hour, and another, and still the rabbi did not come. The elders of the Hasidim saw this, draped their tallitot, wrapped their tefillin, and they recited the morning prayers. They concluded their prayers, but the rabbi still remained in his room. They sat surprised, waiting but saying nothing. When Rabbi Yosef Bunam, the father of the child, and son-in-law of the rabbi, saw that his father-in-law continued to tarry, he could no longer restrain himself. He dared to knock on the door once, twice, in order to arouse him and hurry him. But the rabbi remained inside and did not reply.

The hour of *Minḥa Gedola* arrived, and still, the rabbi did not come out of his room. Not knowing why, the crowd whispered among themselves; they began to worry about the rabbi, but no one dared to enter his holy space. They peeked through the key-hole and saw him sitting immersed in his thoughts, his face glowing. They were frightened and drew back.

At four o'clock in the afternoon, the crowd heard footsteps coming from inside, and then the door opened and the rabbi appeared in the doorway. Immediately, everyone rose in his honor. The rabbi entered the beit midrash, looked around, and asked that the baby be brought to him. Rabbi Levi Yitzhak performed the ritual circumcision, and then took the cup of wine and recited the proper blessing. And when he reached the words, "Blessed are You, *Adonai*, who establishes the covenant," he took some wine on his finger and placed it in the mouth of the baby, and said: "Our

God and God of our ancestors, sustain this child for his father and mother, and may his name be called in Israel, Moshe Yehuda Leib the son of Yosef Bunam."

The father of the baby heard the name pronounced by his father-in-law, and was stunned. He did not know what had caused him to call the baby Moshe Yehuda Leib. Meanwhile, the crowd recited the afternoon Minḥa prayers, and when they finished, they washed their hands and sat down to the mitzva feast.

At the end of the meal, Rabbi Levi Yitzhak turned to his son-in-law Rabbi Yosef Bunam, who was sitting next to him, and said, "My son! I see that you want to ask me a question. Go ahead and ask." Rabbi Yosef Bunam replied, "Yes, my teacher, my master, two things surprised me. Why were you late in coming to the *brit mila*? Is not your custom to be among those who are anxious to fulfill mitzvot as early as possible, especially for the mitzva of circumcision? The second question is, what caused you to name the child, may he live a long life, Moshe Yehuda Leib? This name is not found anywhere in our entire family."

The rabbi said, "Listen carefully while I explain everything to you, and you will know what is ahead of you." Immediately, all those nearby bent their ears to hear the holy rabbi. There was silence in the beit midrash, and Rabbi Levi Yitzhak told the following story:

"Today, I arose early in the morning, planning to bring my dear grandson into the covenant of our father Abraham, peace and blessing be unto him. When the sun rose, I opened the window, and I saw a great darkness in the world, in the heavens above and on earth below. I turned here and there to find out what was going on, and I discovered that one of the righteous of the generation had died and gone to heaven, the holy tzaddik Rabbi Moshe Yehuda Leib of Sassov, son of the famous Rabbi Yaakov of Brody, of blessed memory. I sat in deep sorrow, and tears streamed from my eyes for Israel's rabbi who went to his rest and left us grieving. As I sat in mourning, in great distress, I heard a heavenly voice announce: 'Make room for Rabbi Moshe Yehuda Leib the son of Rabbi Yaakov, and go out to welcome him!' Responding to the announcement, many holy and pure souls gathered to greet the tzaddik of the generation and to bring him into their group with honor. When he arrived in heaven, and was surrounded by tzaddikim and Hasidim, he suddenly heard a voice reverberating from one end of the world to the other. He immediately left the holy community, ran toward the voice, and arrived at the doorstep of *Gehinom*. He entered without permission, and remained there. Everyone waited a long time, but he did not come out.

"The guards of *Gehinom* saw him pacing, walking back and forth as if he were searching for someone, and thought that he had entered by mistake. They approached him and told him that he was in the wrong place, and asked him to leave and go to the place reserved for him in *Gan Eden*. Rabbi Moshe Yehuda Leib listened to their words, but remained silent. They again told him to leave, but he did not reply. He would not move from his place. They were frightened and did not know what to do, whether to force him out or to leave him there as he wished. They decided to ask the rabbinic tribunal on high what to do. But even they did not know how to answer, since there had never been a case like this before, that such a great tzaddik arrived in hell through his own will. And since it was not clear to them what to answer, they decided to bring the case before the Throne of Glory.

"They came before the Throne of Glory and explained that a great tzaddik, Rabbi Moshe Yehuda Leib, son of Rabbi Yaakov, had died, and when he went to the next world, he entered *Gehinom* without permission and refused to leave. The tribunal declared that he must go before the Throne of Glory to explain what had brought him to do this, as it is written, 'A person does not declare himself evil.' A messenger of the tribunal informed Rabbi Moshe Yehuda Leib that that he was summoned to stand before the Throne of Glory, and that he must go immediately. But he was not frightened, and calmly answered: 'My whole life I stood by one mitzva, and dedicated my life to it in the world of lies, and now, that I have an opportunity to do this mitzva in the world of truth, shall I not fulfill it? I will not move from here until I fulfill it, and if it is Your will to hear my arguments, I am ready to explain, but only in this place.'

"The messenger brought his words before the Throne of Glory, and they permitted him to present his arguments as he desired.

"He began: 'Master of the world! You know how great is the mitzva of redeeming captives. After all, because of its importance, You Yourself have fulfilled it, not through an angel or a messenger. When the Jewish people were captive in Egypt, and Pharaoh hardened his heart and did not want to release them from the house of bondage, You Yourself came down, in Your honor and glory, to redeem them.

'I have emulated Your qualities, labored for this mitzva my whole life, and all the captives were fit in my eyes. I did not distinguish between evil ones or righteous ones. They were all beloved to me. Whenever I discovered where they were and who held them captive, I tried to redeem them. I did not rest, nor was I silent, until I could free them. And here in *Gehinom*, I discovered so many captives for whom I desire to fulfill this very mitzva, which is dependent neither on place nor time. And if You say, behold, I am exempt now from the mitzvot? Not at all! I will not move from here until I fulfill this mitzva, since it is clearly known before You that never have I been like servants who serve their master in order to receive a reward. Furthermore, the mitzvot are beloved to me, and I intend to keep them in every place and in every hour, even if there is severe punishment resulting from performing them. So shall I do here, in *Gehinom*.

'If I am able to free the captives, wonderful! And if not, I prefer to remain with them in the fires of hell and to suffer along with them, rather than dwell with the tzaddikim in *Gan Eden*, and to bask in the light of the Divine Presence.'

"Thus stood Rabbi Moshe Yehuda Leib and presented his claim. His words reached the Throne of Glory, and it was if the Blessed Holy One Himself delivered the decision. A heavenly voice announced, 'Great are the tzaddikim who are devoted constantly to others, and great is the mitzva which rewards those who do it, in this world and in the next. And since the merit of this mitzva is great, we should take into account, therefore, how many people Rabbi Moshe Yehuda Leib redeemed in his life, them, their children after them to the end of all generations, and this number of souls he has permission to redeem here too.'

"Immediately the Book of Remembrances was brought and opened, and all the names of the redeemed were counted – their children and their children's children, totaling sixty thousand souls. Immediately, Rabbi Moshe Yehuda Leib was given permission to select sixty thousand from among all the souls in *Gehinom*, and transfer them to *Gan Eden*. Since the choice was up to him, he began to go from room to room. He labored with great effort and found distant souls who had lingered there many years and still did not merit being moved to heaven. It was not an easy task, since those souls were spread out over many sections of *Gehinom*, and he worked very hard to discover souls even in the hidden places.

"After much effort, he gathered all the scattered souls and counted them, and their number was sixty thousand. He took them from *Gehinom* in long lines, with him at the head. And so he brought them to *Gan Eden*.

"Until this tzaddik brought these souls to their final resting place," added Rabbi Levi Yitzhak, "I sat watching him and could not move from my place. Have we not been taught, 'Greater are tzaddikim in death than in life' (Ḥullin 7b)? I saw the greatness of this tzaddik from the moment he entered *Gehinom* until the gates of *Gan Eden* opened before him, and he entered with all his captive souls, sixty thousand in number. And when they all had entered *Gan Eden*, and the gates were locked, I returned to this world, and remembered that I had a *brit mila* to perform.

"I opened the door and found this holy assembly in the beit midrash, waiting impatiently for the *brit*. So I hurried to bring the precious baby, may he live a long life, into the covenant of our father Abraham, may he rest in peace and blessing. And I gave this tender child the name Moshe Yehuda Leib in memory of this holy, pure soul, who died today and went to his eternal reward, may his name be blessed. 'Happy are those tzaddikim, whose lives are filled with blessing and good deeds, both in this world and the next, and who change the quality of judgment to the quality of mercy; not only do they have their own merit, but they also bring merit to others both in their lives and after their deaths. May their merit protect us and all Jews, amen and amen.'"

A Place in the World to Come

It happened once that in Berdichev and in the entire surrounding region there was a shortage of etrogim for Sukkot. Just two days before the festival, the tzaddik of Berdichev, Rabbi Levi Yitzhak, and the entire community were frantic because they did not have an etrog.

Rabbi Levi Yitzhak sent several emissaries in all directions in hopes of meeting someone with an etrog. The emissaries searched and searched, until they finally saw a wagon coming their way. In the wagon was a Jew with an etrog and lulav in his hand. They were overjoyed and stopped the wagon, but their joy did not last long, since the Jew told them that he was not going to Berdichev on this trip, and his home was in a village far from there.

The emissaries continued to press him to stop briefly at the home of the tzaddik of Berdichev, and the Jew was persuaded. When the rabbi saw the Jew with the etrog and lulav, he was filled with joy, and asked the guest to stay in Berdichev for the holiday in order to enable the entire community to perform the mitzva of shaking the lulav. The traveler refused, however, since he had in his household, thank God, a wife and children, and why should he deny himself the happiness of the festival by staying in a foreign city?

In reply, the tzaddik of Berdichev promised him that for the merit of this act he would be rewarded with wealth and worthy children. But the Jew didn't want to hear. He did not want riches, thank God he made a fine living, and he had, thank God, fine, upstanding children. No, he could not remain there; he must be at home for the festival.

Seeing that the Jew was adamant, the tzaddik said to him, "If you fulfill my request, I promise you a place next to me in *Gan Eden.*" When the Jew heard this promise, he immediately relented and agreed to remain. The entire community rejoiced along with the tzaddik of Berdichev, and even the traveling Jew was happy.

The Jew put down the etrog and lulav and went into the city to prepare himself for the festival. At the same time, the tzaddik sent a messenger to all the Jews in the city who had a sukka to tell them, on his orders, not to permit the traveler into their sukkot. They should spare no food and drink, and they should provide the very best they have, but as for entering the sukka, it is forbidden.

Why? No one understood, and no one dared to ask. When the tzaddik orders, the people obey.

That evening, after prayers, the Jew went from the great synagogue to his inn, and entered the room that was assigned to him. There he saw a table beautifully set with candles, wine, *ḥalla*, fish, and everything arranged in beautiful dishes. He was surprised. Why did they set up such a lovely table indoors? Is it possible that the innkeeper, who seemed to be a pious Jew, did not have a sukka?

So he went outside to the courtyard and his eyes brightened with joy. He saw a large sukka, and inside, the innkeeper with his family. He opened the door of the sukka, greeting the man with "*Ḥag Same'aḥ!*" But he was not allowed to enter. He stood in shock, upset and afraid. What was going on? No one answered him. He went to a neighboring sukka , but the same thing happened. He was not allowed to enter. The same thing happened with every sukka. What could be the reason?

Finally, he found out the secret. A firm order had been issued by the tzaddik of Berdichev not to let him enter any sukka. Alarmed, he ran to the tzaddik, and in great sorrow and shame, with tears streaming from his eyes, he asked, "What did I do to cause this? What sin did I commit?"

Rabbi Levi Yitzhak replied that if the traveler really wanted to dwell in a sukka, he would order that he be permitted to enter, but on one condition: that he promise, and affirm with a handshake, to give up his place in *Gan Eden* which he was promised as a reward for the etrog. When he heard this condition, the Jew stood confused. On the one hand, how could he give up such bliss, in the portion promised him in the World to Come, in a place next to the tzaddik of Berdichev in *Gan Eden*? And for what had he therefore been enticed to agree to ruin the joy of his festival, to be apart from his wife and family, and go to a strange place, all for nothing?

On the other hand, how could he agree to violate the mitzva of dwelling in a sukka, which he had been careful to observe his whole life? And how is it possible that while every other Jew was dwelling in a sukka, he would be eating in his room?

He finally overcame his desire and reached out to shake the hand of Rabbi Levi Yitzhak and called out in a loud voice, "I hereby promise, with this handshake, that I give up the place in *Gan Eden*, provided that the rabbi permit me to dwell in a sukka!"

During the whole festival, Rabbi Levi Yitzhak did not speak to him, and only on Shemini Atzeret did the rabbi call him, and sit him down at the head of the table next to him, and extend great honor to him. Then he turned to him and said, "Do not be angry at me, my son, that I treated you so harshly. I did not desire that a Jew acquire a place in the next world for such a cheap price, without effort, doing business just through a handshake.

"A Jew must acquire a place in the World to Come through great effort. A place in the World to Come one must merit through his own good deeds. Because of this, I wanted to test you, to see if you would pass. And now that you have succeeded in passing the test, with God's help, and demonstrated such devotion, giving up the World to Come for the sake of fulfilling the mitzva of sukka, I hereby return to you my previous promise, and give you my word that we will dwell, God willing, in *Gan Eden*, both of us together."

The Reward of a Mitzva

Rabbi Levi Yitzhak of Berdichev once noticed a certain Jew bareheaded, with a long, overgrown shock of hair. He approached him and said, "My son, what made you decide to grow out your forelock like a gentile?"

"My master," replied the man apologetically, "I am an apprentice of a barber, and my work is with officials and landowners, and I must appear suitable to them."

"I will give you a guilder," Rabbi Levi Yitzhak said to him, "if you shave your forelock. Your appearance is violating the biblical law of 'Do not follow their ways' (Lev. 18:3)."

"No, my master," said the apprentice, "I cannot."

Rabbi Levi Yitzhak increased his offer: "I will give you two guilders."

"No," refused the apprentice.

Rabbi Levi Yitzhak increased the offer up to twenty-five guilders, but the apprentice stood firm in his refusal. He simply did not want to ruin his attractive hair.

"If you cut your forelock," said Rabbi Levi Yitzhak, "you will be assured a place in the World to Come."

Immediately the apprentice acquiesced and cut his forelock.

Rabbi Levi Yitzhak raised his eyes to heaven and said: "Master of the universe! Look down from heaven and see, who is like Your people Israel, believers, the children of believers? Even the simple folk are full of faith. This barber's apprentice slaves every day, sweats until he earns one guilder. How much harder must he work to earn twenty-five guilders? And what he refused to do for a reward of twenty-five guilders, he hastened to do for a place in the World to Come, which he never even saw."

Honor in Death

In the city of Uman lived a certain Jew, well thought of in his community, who in his old age sold his possessions and traveled to *Eretz Yisrael*, so he could live out the rest of his days in the Holy

Land and be buried, after one hundred and twenty years, in the soil of the Holy Land.

After a short while, the man decided suddenly to return to Uman. And so he did. Eventually, the citizens of Uman noticed that he had returned to their city. The people were very surprised and could not understand. Questions accumulated from all sides. Why did he go, and then return? What was he thinking when he left, and what was he thinking when he returned? But he was silent and did not reply to anyone. The whole matter was a great mystery to his fellow citizens.

A short time passed and the Jew became ill. He sent for the leaders of the *hevra kaddisha,* saying that he had something urgent to tell them. The men came and he chatted with them about matters of little importance. The leaders were surprised, and left.

The next day, he again sent for the same men. At first, they refused to come, but they relented. Again, the man spoke with them about nothing important. The leaders became angry that he had dragged them there for nothing, and left. On the third day, the sick man sent for them again. This time they did not want to hear from him. He was told that the leaders did not want to come. The sick man then sent word to them that this time he would explain the reason for his invitations. He pleaded with them to come.

The leaders came and sat near the sick man's bed, and he said to them: "The time has come to reveal to you a certain fact about my life. In my youth, I used to travel to different fairs to sell my goods and this is how I made my living. Most of my travels were in the region of Berdichev, and it was my custom that every time I passed near Berdichev I would stop for a day or two to spend time with the tzaddik Rabbi Levi Yitzhak, of blessed memory.

"On one occasion, I was returning from a fair and I passed through Berdichev. I came to the home of the tzaddik, and saw him walking around his room, draped in his tallit, and with great devotion reciting the verses and readings that precede the prayer service. I did not dare enter his room at such a time, so I stood in the next room and listened to his sweet voice.

"Suddenly, there were loud noises and the shouts of several men and women, who opened the door to the rabbi's room and entered while quarreling with one another. They had come to the rabbi for a rabbinic tribunal. They presented their arguments, and I heard the essence of their case:

"A certain poor Jew worked in the business of money-changing. Since he did not have any money of his own to trade with, he would borrow certain sums from his friends, then trade with their funds, earn a bit for himself, pay off his debts, and start all over again. On that particular night, he had lost a sum of three hundred guilders which he had borrowed. There was no end to his sorrow. His livelihood would be gone, and he would be regarded as someone responsible for a bad debt. The man also suspected his servant of stealing the money. She screamed that she had had no part in the theft. The man reviled and reproached her, and even hit her, hoping she would return the money.

"The helper went to her father and mother and told them what had happened, and they arrived at the house of the Jew shouting over the fact that he had hit their daughter. The Jew screamed at the parents and their daughter, until they all decided to go to the rabbi.

"The rabbi listened to their arguments and said, 'I see that the servant is innocent. This man suspected her falsely. But on the other hand, I also see that the man actually lost the money, and did not fabricate the story in order to implicate the servant. Where the lost funds are – to my sorrow I do not know.'

"Suddenly, the tzaddik stood up in the middle of the room and said, 'If I could find someone to give me three hundred guilders to cover this Jew's loss, I would promise him a place in the World to Come.'

"When I heard the words of the tzaddik from behind the door, I went in and said,

"'Will the rabbi put this promise also in writing?'

"'Yes.'

"I immediately took three hundred guilders out of my pocket, and handed them to the tzaddik. The tzaddik gave the money to the Jew, and said to the servant, 'Since you were suspected without justification, I bless you that you will find a proper mate.'

"To the Jew he said, 'You I bless that in the future you will suffer no further loss.'

"Everyone left the tzaddik's home satisfied, and he prepared to recite his prayers. After the recitation of the prayers, I entered the tzaddik's room again and reminded him of his promise regarding the written agreement. He immediately called his servant and ordered him to bring a pen, ink, and paper. The tzaddik wrote a note, placed it in an envelope, sealed it, handed it to me, and said, 'Here is an envelope. Be careful not to open it or read what is written in it during your entire life. When your end comes, and you feel that your time has arrived, hand the envelope to the heads of the *hevra kaddisha* and ask them to place the note in your grave.'

"I was happy to receive the envelope, and of course I was careful not to open it or read its contents. In order to preserve the envelope, I decided to hide it in a special place. I gave my siddur to a bookbinder to re-do the binding, and have the envelope sewn into the binding.

"When I traveled to *Eretz Yisrael*, I forgot, with all the commotion, to take the siddur with me. When I arrived, I remembered that I had left the siddur in Uman. I quickly decided to return to Uman. Now, you will well understand that I was not upset and confused when I returned from the Holy Land. When I became ill, and it seemed to me that my end was near, I sent for you. But when you came, I felt better, and thought that that day was not my last day on earth – so I had to divert your attention. The same thing happened the next time. Today, I feel that my end has truly arrived. Therefore, I am handing you the envelope, and request that you fulfill the words of the tzaddik, and put the envelope into my grave."

The members of the *hevra kaddisha* took the envelope and promised him to fulfill his request. Several hours later the man died.

Afterward, the heads of the *hevra kaddisha* said, "The deceased alone was told that he should not read what is written in the note. But now that he has passed away, there is no reason why we cannot read what the tzaddik wrote."

They opened the envelope and found these words written on the note: "Open for him the gates of *Gan Eden*. Signed, Levi Yitzhak ben Sarah."

The leaders of the *hevra kaddisha* fulfilled their mission, placed the note in the grave of the deceased, and buried him with great honor.

ϫϭ ϫϭ ϫϭ

The Magical Garden of Eden

It was the time of the war between France and Russia (1812). Napoleon I, Emperor of France, attacked Russia, and because of his many mighty victories in his numerous wars he was accorded such glory that he became an almost legendary figure. The Polish aristocrats joined Napoleon's army, and the Jews of Russia saw in this war the realization of the prophetic vision of "the war of Gog and Magog." Yet they differed in their opinions about the exploits of Napoleon. Some thought they would bring good results, and others thought they would bring bad results. This difference of opinion was particularly noticeable among the various hasidic rabbis and their followers. Some prayed for Napoleon's victory, and others prayed for his defeat.

The Hasidim recounted many tales about the dispute between the hasidic tzaddikim regarding this war. The giants in the group of hasidic rabbis, Rabbi Yisrael of Kozhnitz, Rabbi Menahem Mendel of Rimanov, and Rabbi Yaakov Yitzhak of Lublin, united to pray that Napoleon would be victorious, for that would bring redemption to Israel. According to a tradition popular among the hasidic elders, these three masters hoped that Rabbi Levi Yitzhak of Berdichev, who had already passed on to the "world of truth," would stand on their side and, by virtue of his righteousness, see to it that their prayers were accepted and that the redemption of Israel would come hastily.

The Hasidim used to relate that on the Rosh HaShana before his death, the tzaddik of Berdichev turned his eyes to heaven, just before the shofar blasts, and said:

"Master of the universe, Your servant David said before You, 'They stand this day to (carry out) Your rulings, for all are Your servants' (Ps. 119:91), and I, Levi Yitzhak, interpret this verse now as follows: 'They stand this day for Your rulings' – the Jewish people, Your chosen ones, stand today to judge You, as it were, since everything, all the many grueling troubles that we suffer, the difficult and cruel decrees, the slaughters and massacres, all this is only because we are Your servants. And as King David said elsewhere, 'It is for Your sake that we are slain all day long, that we are regarded as sheep to be slaughtered' (Ps. 44:23). Yes, Master of the universe, because of You we are killed and slaughtered, so according to the standards of justice, upon You, as it were, is the duty to save and redeem us speedily."

Then Rabbi Levi Yitzhak turned to all the worshipers in his beit midrash and said, "I promise you that after my death, when

I stand in heaven, I will not rest nor be silent. I will shake worlds, I will summon to a tribunal the entire heavenly host, and I will demand from them the redemption of our people from exile."

Rabbi Hayim Elazar Spira (d. 1937) of Munkatsh gathered his students and told them:

"Rabbi Levi Yitzhak of Berdichev, may his merit protect us, the great defender of Israel, as he lay on his deathbed, before he closed his eyes forever, asked his followers who surrounded his bed: 'Are you not astonished that all the tzaddikim, who in their lives shook heaven and earth to cancel the evil decrees against Israel, are so passive after they reach heaven? Why do they not rattle the Throne of Glory? Where is the tzaddik of Sassov, Rabbi Moshe Leib, who loves the People of Israel so, that the sound of a baby in its crib did not let him rest in the lower world? Where is the holy Baal Shem Tov himself? Why do they not hasten the righteous redeemer to come and bring an end to the suffering of Israel?'

"Not one of his friends dared to reply to his question.

"Rabbi Levi Yitzhak regained his strength and said: 'When a tzaddik goes to heaven, they immediately arrange a place for him in *Gan Eden*. Radiant heavenly angels welcome him with love, grasp him in their arms, and lead him to the sanctuaries of glory. The shining splendor of the sanctuaries and the brilliance of the heavens blind the eyes of the tzaddik. And from the power of the awe, he completely forgets the deep mire of this world and the suffering of the people left behind, sighing and moaning.

'It pains the tzaddik to leave the glowing worlds of the ten spheres for even a minute, and to pay attention to the suffering of mortals. Everything relating to people in this world seems in his eyes as nothingness.'

"Rabbi Levi Yitzhak reflected for a moment and continued: 'Nevertheless, I promise you that my eyes will not be blinded there, and I shall not hover in the heavens in peace and tranquility at a time when down here the Jewish people are in pain and agony, anticipating with impatience the coming of the redeemer. I shall not listen to the voice of the heavenly angels, and I shall not enter *Gan Eden*. I shall stand before the Creator and shake His Throne of Glory. I shall not remain silent until my prayer for the People of Israel is accepted. Only then will I sit with the righteous in the glorious sanctuary."

The rabbi of Munkatsh continued: "When Rabbi Moshe Teitelbaum (d. 1841), the tzaddik of Ujhely, heard what the tzaddik of Berdichev promised before his death, he asked, 'Therefore are you astonished about what happened to the great defender Rabbi Levi Yitzhak? Why is he too mute? Did he not promise that his eyes would not be blinded, that he would rattle the Throne of Glory, and destroy the heavens?'

"Rabbi Teitelbaum answered: When Rabbi Levi Yitzhak died and his soul rose to the heavens, the ministering angels greeted him to bring him to the sanctuaries in *Gan Eden*, as they do for other tzaddikim. But Rabbi Levi Yitzhak demurred and said to them, 'Leave me alone with your *Gan Eden*. You will not blind my eyes. I left below mortals, who are suffering and hurting, and who await the redeemer and the redemption. I want to come before the Throne of Glory, and before the Creator Himself I will present my prayer. I will call Him to a tribunal, and I shall not surrender. I shall not move until an end comes to the dark exile below. Only then can you bring me to *Gan Eden*.'

"A loud noise was heard among the heavenly host. From the time of the creation of *Gan Eden* in the heavens nothing like this had ever transpired. Will the special place in *Gan Eden* of a tzaddik such as Rabbi Levi Yitzhak, remain empty? Are not all the lofty tzaddikim, all the *Tanna'im* and the *Amora'im*, the entire holy congregation of the Baal Shem Tov, waiting for him there? But Rabbi

Levi Yitzhak stood firm: 'I refuse this honor, I shall not enter! I am afraid that the glow and the glory of the sanctuaries will turn my heart from the suffering of those below.'

"What did the heavenly angels do?

"As is well known, Rabbi Levi Yitzhak was well versed in music. He also knew how to play the violin, whose sounds accompanied the melody of his Kaddish, and the *Dudeleh* (a hasidic tune). The heavenly angels went to King David and brought him near to the gate of *Gan Eden*. The 'sweet singer of Israel' (King David) began to play on his harp a chapter from his Book of Psalms, and the sweetness of the melody captured the heart of Rabbi Levi Yitzhak and drew him little by little across the threshold of *Gan Eden*. And the minute the feet of the tzaddik crossed the threshold, his eyes were blinded by the glow of the sanctuaries, and even he, the great tzaddik, forgot us and left us in anguish.

"'But,' said the tzaddik Rabbi Moshe Teitelbaum, 'I, who do not know how to play the violin, I never held one in my hand, King David could not sway me to *Gan Eden*. I will stand outside, and I will prostrate myself before the Creator; my jug of tears I will take with me and pour it out before the Throne of Glory, and I shall not move from there until I hear the footsteps of the redeemer.'"

The rabbi of Munkatsh was silent, halted his visionary story, and was lost in thought.

One of his students rose and asked: "What happened to the tzaddik, Rabbi Teitelbaum, after he himself left this world? Did he not promise that he would not be silent, and would not rest until he heard the footsteps of the redeemer? Why do we still not hear the voice of the messenger, announcing the redemption?"

The rabbi of Munkatsh replied to his students:

"You want to know what happened to the tzaddik, Rabbi Moshe Leib of Ujhely? The gates of *Gan Eden* flew open before him, but he demurred and did not want to enter. The angels pleaded with him but he refused. 'No! My heart does not permit me to roam about in the sea of lights in the company of lofty tzaddikim while there, down below, mortal humans swim in the sea of tears.'

"Again a storm arose in the host of heaven. Is it possible that a tzaddik like Rabbi Moshe Leib, who comes to heaven filled with Torah, mitzvot, and good deeds, will meander outside *Gan Eden*? But once again, the angels on high found a ruse to make Rabbi Moshe Leib forget his promises.

"What did they do? The tzaddik of Ujhely was a great scholar and was accustomed to preach in public for many hours. The angels approached him and told him that inside the gate of *Gan Eden* sits a group of scholars who are expecting to hear some words of Torah from him. A strong urge to preach descended upon Rabbi Moshe Leib. He approached the group and began to present before them new insights, deep ideas, and homilies that everyone was anxious to hear. Even now, he still stands and converses with the heavenly host. And again, not a sign of the end of the exile."

The tzaddik of Munkatsh concluded and said: "Thus all are wandering around heaven, close to the Divine Presence, and forgetting our lowly world below. The holy saints, may their memory be for a blessing, their merit surely will protect us in this world and in the next. But we have only our Father in heaven to rely on, for there is no forgetfulness before His Throne of Glory."

Surrender of the Evil Inclination

A wealthy merchant visited Rabbi Levi Yitzhak of Berdichev to receive a blessing for his business. When he was in the company of the rabbi, the wealthy man removed a box of sniffing tobacco from his pocket. The box was attractive and beautifully engraved.

Rabbi Levi Yitzhak asked to see it. He was impressed and asked if he could have it.

"Of course," answered the rich man.

The rabbi smiled and returned it. "You understand," said the rabbi to the wealthy man, "that I cannot take the box with me to the next world. However, the reward for overcoming 'You shall not covet,' that I will surely take."

Tisha B'Av

Who Needs to, Who Can?

"I wonder, why was it necessary
To command us regarding the fast of Yom Kippur,
And the fast of Tisha B'Av?
After all, on the Holy Day,
The great holiday of forgiveness, pardon and atonement, prayers
      and chants,
Who would need to eat?
Tisha B'Av – the day that is filled with obligation and tragedy,
      mourning and moaning
For the people and the land that were ravaged –
Who can eat?"

Who Is Like Your People, Israel?

It happened that Rabbi Levi Yitzhak of Berdichev was walking in the street on Tisha B'Av. He noticed a Jew eating and drinking in public. He approached him and said, "My son, surely you forgot that today is Tisha B'Av."

"No, Rabbi, I know that today is Tisha B'Av."

"Therefore," continued Rabbi Levi Yitzhak, "you must not know that on Tisha B'Av it is forbidden to eat and drink."

"No, Rabbi," said the man, firm in his opinion, "I know that today is a fast day."

"I am certain," said Rabbi Levi Yitzhak, seeking to vindicate the man, "that you are not well, and observing a fast would endanger your health."

"No, Rabbi," he smiled, "I am very healthy; may all Jews be in such good health."

Rabbi Levi Yitzhak lifted his eyes to heaven and said, "Master of the universe, look down from heaven and see what a wonderful, holy people are Israel. Three times I gave him an opportunity to lie, and still he tells the truth!"

"Alas! Lonely Sits the City"

On the eve of Tisha B'Av, after the final meal before the fast, Rabbi Levi Yitzhak sat immersed in his thoughts, and did not move from his place.

The synagogue attendant approached him and said, "Rabbi, the congregation is waiting for the reading of *Eikha*."

Rabbi Levi Yitzhak lifted his eyes and said, "Indeed, has the Messiah not yet arrived?"

"No," replied the synagogue attendant.

Rabbi Levi Yitzhak rushed to the beit midrash, broke out in a bitter cry, and began: "Alas, lonely sits the city" (Lam. 1:1).

To Sweeten the Bitterness of Life

"The weekly Torah portion of *Parashat Pinḥas* (Num. 25:10–30:1) includes the main ideas of all the festivals. We read this *parasha* on all the biblical festivals, but it is also read regularly during the period of *Bein HaMetzarim*, the three-week period between the two fast days of the Seventeenth of Tammuz and Tisha B'Av.

"Why do we mix joy with mourning?

"The answer is that the holy nation of Israel mourns deeply on these days, during these three weeks, over the fall of Jerusalem, the destruction of the *Beit HaMikdash*, and all the other terrible tragedies that occurred on those days. So that they do not become mired, heaven forbid, in the depths of sadness, we read on those days the portion containing the festivals. The spirit of joy that emanates from it diminishes the bitterness."

Torah

The Evil Inclination Is Outdoors

Several teachers in Berdichev came to Rabbi Levi Yitzhak with this complaint: fewer and fewer people were coming to the beit midrash to listen to the lectures, and instead were visiting the parks.

Rabbi Levi Yitzhak replied, "Were the evil inclination in the beit midrash, and the Talmud in the park, then your complaints would be legitimate. But since the Talmud is in the beit midrash, and the evil inclination in the gardens, why is it surprising that they are outdoors strolling?"

Argument

It happened that Rabbi Levi Yitzhak of Berdichev had an argument with the rabbi of Yartshov, author of the book *Einei Yisrael*, about the philosophy of Hasidism. Rabbi Levi Yitzhak asked, "Do you know the difference between us? You claim that the simple Hasidim, since they do not study, why pray? I argue that since they pray with enthusiasm, why not also study?"

When There Is No Question, There Is No Answer

When Rabbi Levi Yitzhak of Berdichev saw the book *Shulḥan Arukh HaRav*, written by his in-law, Rabbi Shneur Zalman, he was concerned lest, heaven forbid, the author would become proud that he had the merit to write this important book. He presented to Rabbi Shneur Zalman one of the most difficult questions in the laws of forbidden food.

When Rabbi Shneur Zalman received the question, he struggled with it and did not know how to give a clear halakhic reply. At first he said it was kosher, then changed his mind and said it was not kosher, and then went back and forth – kosher, not kosher – until he despaired. And Rabbi Shneur Zalman was greatly pained by this obstacle with which he had been presented.

When Rabbi Levi Yitzhak saw that he was so greatly pained, he revealed that the question was not real, but rather just an example with which to test him.

Rabbi Shneur Zalman replied: "Our sages, of blessed memory, taught, 'A judge delivers a true judgment in perfect truth' (Sanhedrin 7a). Is there a truth that is not perfect truth? Is it possible to have a truth that is false? Rather, when a judgment is truth, when the questioner asks with honesty and sincerity, the one who is asked knows how to reply in perfect truth. But when the basis of the question is false, the answer is blocked from and blurred to the one who replies. When there is no question, there is no answer."

Wonder of Wonders

Rabbi Levi Yitzhak was seventeen years old when he arrived at the yeshiva of Rabbi Shmelke of Nikolsburg to be tested.

Rabbi Shmelke asked him, "Do you know Torah?"

When he heard the word "Torah," Levi Yitzhak's face glowed, and he answered with enthusiasm, "Torah – wonder of wonders."

Rabbi Shmelke assumed that the student was boastful about his Torah knowledge. So he did not accept him as a student in his yeshiva for two years.

Later on, he was accepted as a student, and Rabbi Shmelke became close to him, and very fond of him, and called him "my son." Rabbi Shmelke taught him the revealed, rational meaning of the Torah, and learned from him the wisdom of the mystical, hidden meaning in the Torah.

In his letters, Rabbi Shmelke referred to him as "Rabbi Levi Yitzhak, my student in the simple meanings and my teacher in the mystical meanings."

Heartache

At the end of Yom Kippur in Lvov, Rabbi Levi Yitzhak of Berdichev returned to his inn. He was served food and drink, but he did not eat. His hosts urged him to eat, but he refused.

They asked him why, and he said, "My heart aches." They brought him liquor to soothe his heartache, but still he did not drink. The hosts asked him, "Rabbi Levi Yitzhak, what does his honor request to soothe his heart, we will bring it."

Rabbi Levi Yitzhak replied, "Bring me a volume of the talmudic tractate Sukka. For twenty-six hours, I have not studied Talmud."

They brought him the volume of Sukka, and he stayed up all night studying it.

Treat Them Leniently

A Great Soul Entered the World

Rabbi Yisrael Friedman of Ruzhin (d. 1850), the nephew of the Maggid of Mezritch, would tell this story:

On the day that Rabbi Levi Yitzhak of Berdichev was born, the Baal Shem Tov sat with a group of close associates in his beit midrash and he was in a joyful mood. When he ordered them to bring whiskey and pastries, the students wondered, "What is different about today?" The Baal Shem Tov replied, "Today a great soul entered the world, a holy soul, and this soul will be an advocate for every Jew."

Even the heavenly angels, added Rabbi Yisrael of Ruzhin, rejoiced on that day. They came with Michael, the archangel of the Jewish people, to stand before God to thank Him for the great gift, in the form of the soul of Rabbi Levi Yitzhak of Berdichev, which He gave to His people Israel from His special treasure store. Satan, as the angel Samael, came too, and stood before God and said:

"Master of the world! You have created Michael the archangel, and assigned him to be an advocate for Your people Israel, and to give them the benefit of the doubt at appropriate times. So too did You create me and shouldered me with the task of prosecuting this people and recording all their sins. I have carried out my task faithfully. I have examined every nook and cranny of Jewish homes, and I overlooked not a single transgression, major or minor, large or small, which I did not prosecute before Your tribunal.

"I have battled many times with the archangel Michael, who always tried to silence me, and more than once I had the upper hand. Now You have given Michael a helpmate, Rabbi Levi Yitzhak, who is destined to be the most skilled defender of the Jewish people. And I am left alone, with no one to help or support me. Where shall I turn?"

"What is your request?" asked the Master of the universe.

"What will You grant me, now that I am bereft of help?" answered Satan. "My request is that You provide me with some tzaddikim who will accompany me to seek out the sins of Your people Israel, air them publicly, and help me in my prosecution."

Rabbi Yisrael of Ruzhin added, with a painful sigh and from a shaken soul, "The request of Satan was fulfilled. To my sorrow, these are the tzaddikim who chase after sinners in every generation. Who knows if they mean well or do it with evil intent?"

Rabbi Yisrael of Ruzhin concluded his talk and said, "I had the privilege of knowing Rabbi Levi Yitzhak in my youth, and I know that he was successful in advocating for the Jewish people. He made a special effort, harnessing all his strength, during the Days of Awe. On Rosh HaShana and Yom Kippur, when he had to battle Satan and all his helpers, among whom were, by all appearances, saintly people who helped him in his accusations, even then Rabbi Levi Yitzhak was the victor."

Dealing with the Evil Inclination

Rabbi Levi Yitzhak was told about an elderly Jew who converted and left his religion at age seventy.

Rabbi Levi Yitzhak replied, "See how even the insignificant members of the Jewish people have a wonderful spark of holiness. This converted former Jew struggled with his evil inclination for seventy years! And during all that time he did not want to desert the God of Israel."

Your Sovereignty Is Forever

It happened once that Rabbi Levi Yitzhak noticed a simple Jew, a wagon driver, draped in tallit and tefillin, rubbing tar on the wheels of his wagon. He was doing his work, work that was decidedly unclean, wrapped with holiness.

Rabbi Levi Yitzhak turned to heaven and said, "Master of the world, see how much this Jew loves You. Even when a Jew rubs tar on his wagon wheels, he does not divert his attention away from You, but he recites Your holy name and does not forget Your sovereignty!"

They Are *Baalei Teshuva*

One Rosh HaShana eve, Rabbi Levi Yitzhak awakened early for *Selihot* and went to the synagogue together with his servant. On their way, since the weather was stormy, they took refuge near one of the houses and waited for the rains to subside. Through the window, the servant noticed a group of reckless men sitting around a table, drinking copiously. The servant sighed in sorrow, and said, "How out of control is this generation! On the morning before Rosh HaShana – with the Day of Judgment on the horizon – they sit and get drunk."

The rabbi turned toward his servant in anger and rebuked him, saying, "One must not slander Jews! May they be blessed, since surely they do not enjoy the good things of this world without reciting a blessing. And certainly they say *Birkhot HaNehenin* both before and after their eating and drinking."

The servant turned to listen to the men's conversation, and heard them whispering about a theft they had carried out the evening before. He turned to the rabbi and said, "Listen, Rabbi, they said themselves that they have violated the grave commandment 'You shall not steal.' It is clear that they are a bunch of simple thieves."

When the rabbi heard this his face lit up and he said, "Now it is clear that they are *baalei teshuva*. They know that the Day of Judgment is upon us, and therefore they are confessing to one another for their sins, so that they can enter the Days of Awe with a clean slate."

≫ ≫ ≫

May You Be Inscribed for a Good Year

Samuel Dresner told this story:

It was late at night, on the secular New Year's eve. The students of Rabbi Levi Yitzhak were still studying in the beit midrash. Suddenly, the door of the rabbi's private room opened, and Rabbi Levi Yitzhak came into the beit midrash. "May you be inscribed and sealed for a good year," he called out. He then immediately returned to his room and closed the door behind him.

The Hasidim were shocked. Clearly, the rabbi knew that it was not the new year of the Jews, but only the new year of the gentiles. Why then did he bless them?

After a while, the door opened again and the rabbi repeated the blessing. And after another short while, he did so a third time.

The Hasidim were perplexed. They asked one of the rabbi's longtime close friends to go into his room and ask him to explain this blessing. And this is what Rabbi Levi Yitzhak said, as transmitted by his friend:

"Last Rosh HaShana, the day on which Israel is judged by the Blessed Holy One, the Jews prayed with fervor in the synagogue. Their prayers and the sound of the shofar arose to heaven. The prayers and supplications touched the Blessed Holy One, and He came down from the throne of judgment and sat on the throne of mercy. There He inscribed a decision that the new year would be a year of good health and happiness for the Jewish people.

"When Yom Kippur arrived, and God saw how everyone fasted, cried, and poured out their hearts in prayer, God lifted His pen in order to seal His decision, judging the People of Israel favorably.

"At that very moment, Satan appeared and registered a complaint. 'Yes, Sovereign of the world,' argued Satan, 'on Yom Kippur they fast and repent, and wear white garments like the angels, but what about the rest of the year, when they are full of sins and evil acts?'

"So the favorable decision was not sealed.

"When the Jewish people began to build sukkot, the defending angel argued, 'Almighty God, do You not see the sukkot, which even the impoverished of Your people are building with joy, in order to fulfill Your mitzvot? For You they are building them. Please seal Your favorable decision.'

"The decision would have been sealed, had not Satan objected once again. 'Yes, Sovereign of the world, for Your sake they are building sukkot – flimsy sukkot made of branches and boards, sukkot which are here today and gone tomorrow. But for themselves – for their homes, their businesses, and entertainment – they create buildings of stone, bricks, and glass, strong and solid, which stand forever.'

"Then came Simhat Torah. The Jews embraced the Torah scrolls, danced, and rejoiced with them in the synagogues.

Again, the defending angel asked God to seal the lenient judgment. 'See now, Almighty God, how Your children rejoice with Your Torah.'

"But Satan intervened: 'Yes, during one evening they dance joyously with Your Torah, their hands stretched out toward You, and their spirit uplifted because of the spirits they drank. But when they are sober and their heads are clear, do they fulfill the mitzvot written in Your Torah?'

"The lenient decision was not sealed.

"And so it happened that the lenient decision which was written in the merit of the Jewish people on Rosh HaShana remained unsealed on Yom Kippur and on Hoshana Rabba, and during many weeks, until this very evening.

"And so, when the gentile new year began, and with it began the drinking, screaming, and quarrels which generally take place on this night, the defending angel approached God and said, 'Sovereign of all the earth, look how they begin the first night of their new year. Please listen to the shouts of pain and the sounds of mischief. Watch the corruption and licentiousness – and remember how Your children began the new year on Rosh HaShana, with prayer, repentance, and holiness.'

"To this argument, Satan had no reply.

"Thus, after postponement of several months, the Blessed Holy One finally sealed the decision which judges the Jewish people with merit.

"Therefore," Rabbi Levi Yitzhak summed up, "I blessed you this evening with the traditional Jewish blessing, "*Leshana tova tikatevu vetehatemu.*"

Tzaddik

His Garment

A certain Hasid once boasted to Rabbi Aharon the Great of Karlin that he knew Rabbi Levi Yitzhak of Berdichev.

Rabbi Aharon said to him, "You are mistaken. You do not know the tzaddik Rabbi Levi Yitzhak. You apparently know only his garment, his outermost layer. But of Rabbi Levi Yitzhak himself, the great tzaddik, you have no clue."

How Fortunate Are We!

The Seer of Lublin (Rabbi Yaakov Yitzhak Horowitz, d. 1815) would set aside an hour every day to thank and praise the Blessed One for bringing into this world the great and holy soul of Rabbi Levi Yitzhak of Berdichev.

The Scent of a Tzaddik

The tzaddik Rabbi Hayim Sanz (d. 1876) once traveled through a certain village. Suddenly, he ordered the driver to stop. The tzaddik descended from the carriage, entered a hotel, and asked if there were any elderly people there. He was told that the hotel owner had an elderly mother, who was ninety years old. The tzaddik asked to see her.

When the elderly woman came he asked her, "Did a tzaddik ever stay in this hotel?"

She replied that once the holy rabbi, Rabbi Levi Yitzhak of Berdichev, of blessed memory, stayed in this hotel for two weeks on his way to Hungary.

The tzaddik told his Hasidim: "As I passed through the village, I sensed a lovely scent of a tzaddik, and I was quite surprised. How did a tzaddik pass through here? Now I understand where this beautiful scent came from, since the holy rabbi of Berdichev was here."

১৯ ১৯ ১৯

God Decrees, a Tzaddik Annuls

"Why is the Creator called 'King of the kings of the kings!?'
This is the matter: A tzaddik, who rules with the fear of God,
The Blessed Holy One decrees – and a tzaddik annuls.
It turns out that the tzaddik is able to rule over the Blessed One,
Since he rules with his fear.
But his rule is itself from the Creator,
Who gives him the strength to annul His decrees.
And in this vein, the tzaddik is called a king,
Because he rules over the Blessed Creator to annul His decrees,
Since He gives strength to the tzaddikim who are called kings.
'Who are the kings? The rabbis.'

180

Because of this, the Blessed Creator is called
'King of the kings of the kings,'
Since He rules over the rulers of the rabbis,
Who have sovereignty over the Blessed Creator."

"I am Unworthy"

"Generally speaking, a tzaddik is always unworthy in his own eyes,
And always in his own mind feels as though he has not even begun
    his work.
And this is the essence of his work, that he always remain humble
    in his own eyes."

Tzedaka

For Your Sake

"A Jew who earns a good living, what does he do?
He raises children to Torah, spends extra on his *oneg Shabbat*
and *Yom Tov*,
Spends more on *hiddur mitzva*,
Is very generous with *tzedaka*,
And most of his expenses are for the performance of mitzvot and
good deeds.
This is why on Rosh HaShana and all the Days of Awe, we say
this prayer:
'Remember us for life – for Your sake, living God.'
All of our energy is totally for Your sake, O God,
So that we can worship You,
And observe Your mitzvot and live for Your sake."

Begging

We do not know a lot about the life of Rabbi Levi Yitzhak in the
home of his father-in-law, Rabbi Yisrael Peretz, the wealthy agent

of the cruel Polish baron, but it is clear that he witnessed a great deal of suffering there. Rabbi Yisrael Peretz was a leading Jew who ran his household generously. He distributed much *tzedaka* to the needy, and the poor would crowd around him to receive regular allotments on an appointed day of the week.

It seems that Rabbi Levi Yitzhak was in charge of distributing the *tzedaka*, and he became close to the poor and the needy. He became involved in their community, bore their burdens, and promoted their claims.

Not long afterward, the wealthy Rabbi Yisrael Peretz lost his fortune and went bankrupt. Because of his large debt to the Polish nobleman, he was sentenced to life imprisonment. At the time, a landlord was permitted to do with a Jewish debtor as he pleased – throw him into a murky pit, make him dance like a bear, abuse him as he wished, and maybe even take his wife and children as servants.

Rabbi Levi Yitzhak's wife, Perel, who was known for her righteousness and her beauty and who knew many languages, influenced the baron with her charm and gentle speech to postpone the payment of the debt – ten thousand guilders – for two years. Meanwhile, Rabbi Levi Yitzhak took to the road with his cane and knapsack, traveling around the area to collect donations and to encourage compassionate Jews to perform the mitzva of redeeming captives.

Rabbi Levi Yitzhak's effort in collecting *tzedaka* was not successful.

Rabbi Levi Yitzhak, who had refused to receive payment all his life, who never used his high position for selfish purposes, was forced by circumstances to beg door to door for funds from wealthy Jews. His hand, accustomed to give, was now extended to receive. His holy mouth, which always delivered complaints to the Master of the universe, was forced to deliver his pleas to flesh and blood.

It seems probable that the eminent family of Yisrael Peretz did not look favorably on the young Rabbi Levi Yitzhak, husband of their beautiful and learned daughter Perel, who in no way looked or behaved as one of the wealthy or influential and, instead, consorted with simple Jews as if he were one of them. Furthermore, he could always be found together with the poor, the needy, and the indigent who gathered near the home of the baron, week after week, to receive the charity that he dispensed.

On the other hand, one can assume that Rabbi Levi Yitzhak, who by nature befriended simple people, conducted himself in humility and received everyone with a pleasant smile and a generous heart. At the home of his wealthy father-in-law he acquired deep wisdom and gained some expertise in the suffering of the poor, who poured out their misery before him and shared with him all the secrets of their battered souls, their humiliation, and their numerous worries. For him, the home of Yisrael Peretz served as a school for the study of the soul and a kind of workshop for increasing his love of Israel.

≥ò ≥ò ≥ò

When a Mitzva Presents Itself, Don't Put It Off

Rabbi Levi Yitzhak of Berdichev once visited a hasidic rabbi to ask him to accompany him to the homes of some wealthy individuals to collect a sum of money for an urgent and worthy cause. The rabbi indicated to Rabbi Levi Yitzhak with a hand signal that the matter would have to wait until he concluded his daily recitation of Psalms, as he was in the middle and could not stop.

Rabbi Levi Yitzhak said to him, "This poor man is swimming in a sea of trouble, and you are reciting Psalms? The Blessed Holy One has tens of thousands of ministering angels who recite Psalms, songs, and praises to Him, but this poor man – if we don't hurry to help him in his hour of crisis, who will? Please stop your recitation of Psalms and come with me right away."

א$ א$ א$

Neglect It One Day – It Will Neglect You Two

At the celebration of the wedding of Rabbi Levi Yitzhak's granddaughter and the son of Rabbi Shneur Zalman of Liadi, Rabbi Levi Yitzhak said to Rabbi Shneur Zalman:

"Dear in-law, since we have been privileged by the Blessed One to arrange this wedding in a happy and successful hour, it is appropriate that we perform some mitzva together."

Rabbi Shneur Zalman agreed, and asked, "Which mitzva?"

Rabbi Levi Yitzhak replied, "*Barukh Hashem* that a mitzva has presented itself to us. I raised an orphan in my home who is now of marriageable age, but I do not have any funds for her wedding. If you agree we can go together to collect funds for *hakhnasat kalla*."

Rabbi Shneur Zalman replied, "Even though I am a stranger in this community, I am most willing to accompany the rabbi of Berditchev."

Rabbi Levi Yitzhak continued, "I have one condition, however, my dear in-law. You cannot become angry with anyone, even if he is wealthy, who contributes a small gift that is not worthy of two rabbis – one of whom is the author of *Tanya*, and the other the local chief rabbi. And please do not say that this is a slight to your honor, heaven forbid."

There was in Berdichev a certain wealthy moneychanger who gave *tzedaka* generously to every poor person, and particularly to worthy poor people and to Torah scholars. Rabbi Levi Yitzhak brought Rabbi Shneur Zalman to this generous man first so they would have a good beginning, since success breeds success.

Rabbi Levi Yitzhak heaped much praise on this wealthy man. But to their great surprise, not only did the rich moneychanger not welcome them warmly, but he gave Rabbi Levi Yitzhak only a small coin, less than a guilder. Rabbi Levi Yitzhak accepted the coin and thanked the man. However, Rabbi Shneur Zalman did not hide the anger in his heart.

When they left the house, Rabbi Shneur Zalman spoke with bitterness to Rabbi Levi Yitzhak: "Is it fitting to give a coin worth less than a guilder to the rabbi of the city, who is requesting a contribution for arranging a wedding? Is this how he shows honor to the Torah?"

Rabbi Levi Yitzhak replied, "Dear in-law, did we not agree between us that you would not become angry at anyone, no matter how much he gave? The city of Berdichev has many charitable donors. Let us go to others. With God's help, we will reach our goal."

When they had walked a few steps from the house of the moneychanger they heard a voice calling to them, "Wait, rabbis, wait!" The wealthy moneychanger ran after them and gave them ten guilders, and also asked for their forgiveness. He explained that for some reason he was confused when they came, and mistakenly had given them a small coin, which was an insult to their important positions, heaven forbid.

Rabbi Levi Yitzhak happily thanked him, and said, "To err is human. Heaven forbid that you should think that a mistaken insult would be considered malicious."

When the moneychanger left, Rabbi Shneur Zalman repeated in pent-up anger, "Is the rabbi of Berdichev placated by ten guilders from one who is asked to assist in the mitzva of organizing a wedding?"

Rabbi Levi Yitzhak replied, "Dear in-law, did we not both agree that you would not become angry at anyone? Let us go visit some others."

After they had walked a few steps further they again heard a voice behind them: "Wait, rabbis, wait!" The wealthy money-changer ran after them and held out a bill of one thousand guilders. Again, he begged forgiveness. Because of spiritual worries he had acted, heaven forgive him, frivolously toward two of the great lights of Israel, and contributed toward arranging a wedding an amount that was a clear insult to their honor.

With the permission of these two wise, outstanding tzaddikim, he wished to relate to them the explanation of the matter, and to ask them to judge him leniently. He had been befuddled and confused. It was embarrassing to tell what had happened, as though his common sense had left him. It was difficult to explain the reason, but he requested of the two great tzaddikim forgiveness and pardon.

Rabbi Levi Yitzhak's face glowed with joy, and he said "His honor is forgiven. We forgive his honor with a full heart. May it be that from now on your honor will be generous to everyone, as he always was."

When the moneychanger left the third time, Rabbi Levi Yitzhak told Rabbi Shneur Zalman this story:

"A few weeks ago, a poor man approached the moneychanger to ask for some *tzedaka*. At that moment, he was involved in a transaction with a few distinguished merchants and paid scant attention to the poor man, who was a worthy man whom one does not dismiss with small coins.

"He gave him a small coin from his pocket. The recipient became angry and threw the coin in his face. When the money-changer saw this, he developed a grudge in his heart toward all beggars who came to him with their burdens, and decided not to give to any beggars – whoever they might be – more than a small coin. A second beggar, who came afterward, also refused to accept the small coin since he was accustomed to receiving more.

"Of course, as tradition states, one transgression brings another in its train. So in the last few weeks, he did not give any money to the poor. What tradition says about the holy Torah applies to *tzedaka* as well: 'If you neglect it one day, it will neglect you two days.' There was concern that this wealthy contributor would habitually come to harden his heart to the poor. Therefore, honorable rabbi, it was appropriate that the author of the *Tanya* and the rabbi of Berdichev agree to accept from him a token contribution, in order to reinvigorate his generosity.

"So we see the power of a deed. Because of the small coin that he gave us at first, his *yetzer hatov* was strengthened to appease us with a gift of ten guilders, and he went from strength to strength, until he was encouraged to allocate to us a thousand guilders for the bride."

Sodom and Gomorrah

Rabbi Levi Yitzhak arranged with the leaders of his city that, in order not to distract him from Torah study, they would not invite him to any meeting that dealt with municipal issues, other than drafting new regulations which required Torah knowledge.

Some weeks after the agreement was made, he was invited to a meeting. Rabbi Levi Yitzhak said to those gathered, "What new law are you planning to enact in the city?" They replied, "Different groups of poor people from the surrounding villages are flooding our city and depriving our poor from *tzedaka*. We would like to enact an ordinance that the poor from outside our city cannot come here to collect charity until the poor of our city have filled their needs. Have not our sages taught and decreed (Bava Metzia 71a), 'The poor of your city take precedence over the poor of another city'?"

Rabbi Levi Yitzhak argued, "Why was it necessary to invite me to this meeting? This law that you propose is not new at all. The members of the 'Four Lands' already enacted that law."

The leaders thought that the rabbi's reference was to the Council of the Four Lands (the central body of Jewish authority in Poland from 1580 to 1764). They said to him, "We have reviewed all the notebooks of rules of the Council of Four Lands, and we did not find this new law which we are now going to enact."

Rabbi Levi Yitzhak replied: "The 'Four Lands' which I mentioned are not the Council of the Four Lands of recent generations in Eastern Europe. Instead, I referred to an ancient law of the original 'Four Lands': Sodom and Gomorrah, Admah and Zeboiim (Gen. 14:8). Did they not decree that the poor and needy would not set foot in their city, as we learn in *Pirkei DeRabbi Eliezer* (ch. 25), 'In Sodom they decreed, whoever gives a piece of bread to the poor, the needy, or the stranger shall be burned'?"

The Power of *Tzedaka*

Rabbi Levi Yitzhak of Berdichev once attended a *seudat mitzva*, where he encountered one of the wealthy citizens of the city – a man who had a reputation as a miser, who clenched his fist whenever an opportunity for *tzedaka* presented itself. Rabbi Levi Yitzhak approached the man and began to reprimand him about holding back from the mitzva of *tzedaka*, which can atone for every sin and transgression.

The wealthy man interrupted the words of the tzaddik of Berdichev, and called out with arrogance: "I have a less expensive way to atone for sins and transgressions. Have not the ancient sages taught that prayer in our day takes the place of animal sacrifices, which atoned for Israel's sins, as it is written, 'Instead of bulls, we will offer the words of our lips' (Hos. 14:3)? You should know that I am fastidious with my daily prayer. From the time I was old enough, I never missed a single prayer in a *minyan*."

"May you be blessed," called Rabbi Levi Yitzhak in a heartfelt voice. "But the truth is that our sages, of blessed memory, who determined that we should substitute prayer for sacrifice, only meant it to apply to the *korban tamid*, the daily sacrifice. But the *korban ḥova*, which one must offer in order to atone for one's sins, can't be compensated for through prayer, but rather through deeds of *tzedaka* and kindness, as it is written in the Book of Daniel (4:24), 'Redeem your sins by beneficence and your iniquities by generosity to the poor.'

"Not only that, but it is appropriate that acts of *tzedaka* precede all prayer, as we learn in the Talmud (Bava Batra 10a), 'Rabbi Eliezer would give a coin to a poor person, and afterward recite his prayers, as it is written (Ps. 17:15): As for me, I shall behold Your face in righteousness.' As Rashi interprets this verse, 'in righteousness' means in acts of *tzedaka* first, and afterward 'I shall behold Your face,' in prayer."

Giving Comes First

Rabbi Levi Yitzhak of Berdichev traveled around to nearby villages to collect funds for a bride, who was the daughter of a prominent man.

One day he chanced upon a certain rabbi who, when he heard the purpose of Rabbi Levi Yitzhak's visit, blessed him that the Blessed One be at his side, and that the needy Jew should merit to arrange a wedding for his daughter with abundance.

Rabbi Levi Yitzhak turned to him and said, "The Torah teaches us (Gen. 14:18–19): 'And King Malkitzedek, king of Shalem, brought out bread and wine … and he blessed him.' First, 'he brought out bread and wine,' and only afterward, 'and he blessed him.'

"First one must give, and only afterward extend blessings."

Yom Kippur

Remembered for a Blessing

Every Yom Kippur eve Rabbi Yisrael Friedman of Ruzhin used to tell stories about Rabbi Levi Yitzhak of Berdichev. He explained that there is special merit in doing this, as it sweetens harsh judgments.

His son, Rabbi Avraham Yaakov Friedman, the first rabbinic leader of Sadigura (d. 1883), added this: "Just by virtue of mentioning the name of the city of Berdichev, the merit of the tzaddik Rabbi Levi Yitzhak helps in granting our requests. And the proof is in the Mishna (Mishna Yoma 3:1): 'The one who saw would say: The entire east has lit up... even to Hebron.' Rashi explains, in the name of the Jerusalem Talmud, 'In order to remember the merit of our ancestors, we mention Hebron.'"

A Pure Prayer

Rabbi Levi Yitzhak of Berdichev explained that the words of the prayer, "Remove Satan from before us and from behind (after) us," are connected to Yom Kippur eve and to Purim. On these two days,

Satan comes to accuse the Jewish people. On Purim, he comes shouting in anger, "Why do Jews drink and get drunk and have fun?" We answer him "from before us," and remind him about the day before Purim – the Fast of Esther – on which we fast all day, recite prayers, and increase our giving of *tzedaka*.

On Yom Kippur eve, he comes again with a similar accusation: "Why do Jews eat and drink so much?" We answer him "from behind (after) us," reminding him of the day after Yom Kippur eve – the long, difficult day of Yom Kippur itself.

This Is My Atonement

It was the custom in Berdichev to delay the recitation of *Kol Nidrei* until nightfall, even though, according to law, it should be recited while it is daylight. This custom originated with Rabbi Levi Yitzhak, who, on Yom Kippur eve, would visit his neighbors and ask each one for a piece of cake as a gift, because of the possibility that they were liable to be punished, God forbid, having to go begging from door to door. By doing this, giving a piece of cake as a gift, they were atoning for a sin they may have committed.

All the people in the community of Berdichev continued to follow this custom.

Say a Good Word

It happened once on the eve of Yom Kippur that Rabbi Levi Yitzhak turned toward heaven and said: "Master of the universe, You see that I am getting old, and weak, and I have in my hand a large *mahzor* with many pages of prayers. I muster my strength and recite all the prayers in this entire *maḥzor*, and ask for Your pardon and forgiveness.

"And You, Master of the universe, are a powerful champion. You have only to recite a single phrase – 'I forgive.'

"Therefore say this one phrase, and it will be a good year."

Why Do You Complain About Us?

On one Yom Kippur night, Rabbi Levi Yitzhak of Berdichev stood before the open holy ark, and said: "Master of the universe! Why do You complain about our sins and transgressions? It is well known to You that all the sins of Your people must fall on the head of a goat, as it is written, 'Thus the goat (Hebrew: *se'ir*) shall carry on it all their iniquities to a land that is cut off' (Lev. 16:22). The 'head of a goat' – that is Esau, who is called 'man of Seir.' It was Esau's persecution of Jacob that caused our sins and iniquities.

"Master of the universe! Who knows better than You that all the sins of Israel can be ascribed to 'a land that is cut off' – the bitter and harsh exile of the sons of Esau (Rome)? Save us please from the hand of my brother Esau."

My Heart Is Exalted

It was Rabbi Levi Yitzhak's custom to lead the prayers on the Days of Awe. Once on the night of Yom Kippur, the congregation stood with their tallitot draped on their shoulders and, though the sun was setting, Rabbi Levi Yitzhak stood in his place, silently immersed in his thoughts.

The congregation was puzzled, but no one dared to say anything to the rabbi, until one man spoke out and protested in a loud voice, and said, "Even with his exalted position, the rabbi must follow the law – and according to the law, the proper time for reciting *Kol Nidrei* is before sunset." Rabbi Levi Yitzhak replied, "You are right," and began to chant *Kol Nidrei*.

When the prayer concluded, the man approached the rabbi and, crying bitterly, begged forgiveness for being so brash.

Rabbi Levi Yitzhak replied: "May you live a long life and be blessed with a good year, since were it not for you, who knows when I would have found myself fit to recite *Kol Nidrei* as the *sheliah tzibbur*? The *yetzer hara* came and enticed me unto arrogance, and said I am high and exalted, as all the citizens of Berdichev came to me to ask for a blessing on Yom Kippur eve. And though I am aware that I am nothing but Levi Yitzhak ben Sarah, the simplest of the simple, the *yetzer hara* succeeded, in a devilish act, and my arrogance overcame me – and an arrogant person is not worthy to serve as *sheliah tzibbur* before the Sovereign of sovereigns, the Blessed Holy One.

"But when you spoke up and protested that even a righteous rabbi must follow the law, I remembered my little worth, who I am and what I am, and I felt worthy to begin to chant *Kol Nidrei*."

Rabbi Levi Yitzhak concluded, "It is proper and fitting that every *sheliah tzibbur* should remind himself of this before he begins to lead the congregation in prayer."

Advocate

On the eve of Yom Kippur, as the sun was setting, and the entire congregation was standing in the synagogue awaiting the *Kol Nidrei*, Rabbi Levi Yitzhak began to walk around the synagogue, from one bench to another, looking all around as if he were searching for something. The congregation stood and looked puzzled.

"What are you searching for, master, at this late hour?"

Rabbi Levi Yitzhak answered, "I am searching for a certain Jew who became inebriated, or drank too much today. I am searching but cannot find such a person."

He immediately stood at the rostrum, and began, as he always did, to plead before God and list the many merits of the Jewish people, and said: "Lord of the world, look at the Jewish people, whom You have chosen for Yourself, a special people, whom You have sanctified with Your mitzvot. Just as You have commanded us to fast on Yom Kippur, so have You commanded us to eat and drink in abundance on Yom Kippur eve. As Your holy sages have taught (Berakhot 8a), 'Whoever eats and drinks on the ninth (of Tishrei) is credited as if he fasted on the ninth and tenth.'

"Had You commanded a mitzva like this to the nations of the world, a mitzva of eating and drinking just before a day of fasting, repentance, and prayer, I am certain that toward evening most of them would be lying about, inebriated, and You would not find one of them coming at sunset to the house of worship. But the Jewish people have done as You have commanded. They ate and drank abundantly and had a great feast, and now just before sunset they have all rushed to the synagogue, and not one is drunk. They are all ready and willing to accept upon themselves the fast of the holy day, to confess before You, and to return to You in truth with a whole heart. Have You found another nation like this in whom there is the spirit of God? And what do the Jewish people ask of You? Just one spoken word and but a few written words. Please say, '*Salaḥti*' (I have forgiven). And please inscribe all the children of Your covenant 'for a good life.'"

May It Be Your Will

A certain woman used to come to Berdichev on Yom Kippur in order to pray in the congregation of Rabbi Levi Yitzhak, and to hear him chant *Kol Nidrei*.

It happened once that she was late, and when she arrived at the synagogue it was already dark. She was deeply sad because she was certain that the evening prayer had already been completed. But Rabbi Levi Yitzhak had not yet begun to lead the congregation in prayer. He was waiting, to the astonishment of the congregation, until she would arrive.

When the woman saw that they had not yet begun to recite *Kol Nidrei*, her heart filled with great joy and she called out to the God of heaven: "Master of the world, how can I bless You for this great favor which You have done for me? May it be Your will that You derive from all Your children as much happiness as I had just now!"

Immediately, there was an opportune moment before God, and supreme loving-kindness covered the world.

❧ ❧ ❧

The Man Who Forgave God

It happened once that Rabbi Levi Yitzhak came to the beit midrash on the night of Yom Kippur. He paced to and fro, but did not begin the recitation of *Kol Nidrei*. At the same time, he noticed a man sitting on the ground in the corner, crying.

Rabbi Levi Yitzhak said to him, "Why do you cry so?"

The man replied: "Rabbi, how can I not cry? Yesterday I had everything, and today I am forlorn, and lacking everything. Lest the rabbi think that I did not behave properly, it is not so. I sat in my village, and whoever came to my door, I gave him food and drink, and whoever came to me hungry went away satiated. And my wife would behave with even more kindness than I. She would walk around the village to see if there was anywhere a poor Jew who needed to be fed.

"And now, the One above came and took my wife from me, and she died. And if this were not enough, He burned down my house, so that I am left bereft of my wife and with no home. And I have six small children. I also had a large siddur with all the *piyyutim* (liturgical poems) and prayers marked so that I did not have to turn the pages to find a single prayer. This too was burned. So how can I forgive Him?"

Immediately, the rabbi ordered him to search the beit midrash for a similar siddur. He searched and found one. The man sat and turned page after page to see if this siddur was ordered like the one that had been burned. It took him about an hour, and during that entire time the rabbi stood and waited.

Finally the rabbi said to him, "Now can you forgive God?" The man answered, "Now I can forgive Him."

Then the rabbi approached the pulpit and began to recite *Kol Nidrei*.

≈≈≈

Mutual Forgiveness

It happened once on Yom Kippur eve toward evening that Rabbi Levi Yitzhak of Berdichev stood at the pulpit to recite *Kol Nidrei*. However, a whole hour crept by and still Rabbi Levi Yitzhak stood quietly. Meanwhile the hour was getting late, the sun was setting, and soon it would be too late.

Suddenly, Rabbi Levi Yitzhak turned to face the congregation and asked the *shamash*, "Is Berel the tailor here in the beit midrash?"

"No, Rabbi," answered the *shamash*.

"Go call him!" ordered Rabbi Levi Yitzhak.

The *shamash* went and brought Berel to the beit midrash.

"Berel," asked Rabbi Levi Yitzhak, "why are you delaying the prayers?"

"What can I do, Rabbi," answered Berel, "if I have no one before whom I can invite God to a tribunal? To the contrary, if the rabbi would like to be the judge, I would consent."

"Let us hear," said Rabbi Levi Yitzhak, "present your grievances."

So Berel the tailor began:

"This is the story, Rabbi. Several days before *Selihot*, the landowner summoned me to sew a new fur coat for him for the winter. I took all my tools, scissors, and an iron, and I went to the court, and the landowner gave me some of the best skunk skins to make him a fine fur coat.

"I thought in my heart, here I am a poor, indigent Jew, and I have a daughter to marry off, and I don't have any funds. I'll cut off the remainder of about ten skunk skins, and I'll have the beginning of a dowry for my daughter. And so I did. I sewed a proper fur coat for the landowner, and I left the remainder of ten skunk skins for myself.

"After I finished the work and began to get ready to return home, I tore out the soft inside from a loaf of bread, and hid the skunk hides there. I put the parcel on my back and began my trip home. After a few miles, I heard a horseman chasing me. I became frightened, so I hid the parcel under a tree, and sat down on the grass, waiting for the horseman.

"'Berel, come back,' called the horseman to me, 'the landowner needs you!'

"I returned to the landowner and was scared to death. Who knew what fate awaited me?

"'Berel,' the landowner said to me. 'Is this the way a skilled craftsman completes his work? After all, you did not sew a hook for me to hang my fur coat!'

"So I gave praise and thanks to the Master of the universe for the miracle which He performed for me. Then I prepared a hook for the fur coat, and continued on my way.

"I returned to the tree – and my parcel with the loaf of bread and the skunk skins was not there! I looked all over, and nothing! I sat down on the ground and began to mull over the matter in my mind. It occurred to me that all this had come from God, as it were. He did not want me to steal the skunk skins from the landowner.

"'If that is the case,' I said to myself, 'if You, Master of the universe, can perpetrate this act against me like this, I no longer desire to continue to labor for You. And I do not desire to continue any more to be a God-fearing person!'

"So I went home, and my wife came to greet me: 'Berel, wash your hands, and have some dinner.' But to spite Him, I sat down and ate without ritual washing. I ate and was satisfied, but did not recite Grace after Meals, and did not recite the evening prayer. I lay down to sleep without reciting the *Shema*. The next morning, the same thing. I did not pray or recite Grace. The days of *Seliḥot* arrived, and I did not rise for *Seliḥot*. On Rosh HaShana, I did not go to pray, I did not hear the blowing of the shofar. In short, if He could do this to me, and anger me in this way, I did not want to have any dealings with Him!

"But now, it is Yom Kippur eve, and we must forgive everyone, and I must also forgive the Master of the universe, since He too forgives everyone. I decided in my heart, all right, I will forgive Him, but on one condition – that He, the Master of the universe, forgive on this day all the transgressions, even the ones, as we know, for which Yom Kippur does not atone! If He forgives everything, I will also forgive Him. But if not, then I will not agree. Just the opposite. Rabbi, make a halakhic decision, am I not right?"

Rabbi Levi Yitzhak lifted his eyes to heaven and said: "Master of the universe. I, Levi Yitzhak the judge, make a halakhic decision that Berel the tailor is right. Berel the tailor forgives You, but You, for Your part, must forgive all the transgressions, sins, and iniquities of the entire nation of Israel!"

Thus in joy and in song, Rabbi Levi Yitzhak turned to the pulpit and began to recite *Kol Nidrei*.

A Blessing Not in Vain

On what basis do we recite in the *Shemoneh Esreh* of Yom Kippur, "Blessed are You, Sovereign, who forgives and pardons"? How can we be certain that the Blessed One truly forgives us, and that this blessing, heaven forbid, is not a blessing in vain?

Rabbi Levi Yitzhak answered: "We say this certainly with an intended goal. A wise child does the same thing. When he wants his father to give him an apple, and he is not certain if his father will give it to him, what does he do? He quickly recites in a loud voice, 'Borei peri ha'etz'. Then he begins to cry out, 'Nu, Oh!' – namely, that it is forbidden to interrupt between the blessing and the eating! At that moment, the father must give the apple to him, since he will not let his son commit a transgression by reciting a blessing in vain, because of an apple.

"We Jews do the same thing with our Father in heaven. We quickly make the blessing, 'Blessed are You … who forgives and pardons,' so God is compelled to do our will and forgive us, since He does not want His children, millions of Jews, to recite a blessing in vain!"

Yitgadal VeYitkadash

All year long, Rabbi Levi Yitzhak of Berdichev laid out all the complaints of the Jewish people against God, but especially during the High Holy Days. During those days of judgment, when it is a mitzva for every Jew to ask forgiveness from the Creator for sins committed before Him, Rabbi Levi Yitzhak chose to bring the arguments of the Jewish people to the heavens, and to plead in their favor with all his might.

Rabbi Levi Yitzhak was gifted with a sweet voice, and he himself led the prayers during the Days of Awe. It happened once, on Yom Kippur, just before the *Musaf* prayer, that Rabbi Levi Yitzhak stood on bended knee next to the holy ark, while his whole body was "shaking and fearful of the One whom Israel praises" (from the prayer for the *sheliaḥ tzibbur*). Rabbi Levi Yitzhak stood like that for a long time. The beit midrash was silent, the worshipers stood tensely, their tallitot draped on their shoulders, looking forward with bated breath to the Kaddish of their rabbi. But the rabbi was silent. With a broken and dispirited heart, he stood with trembling feet, and was filled with thoughts of regret for the "sins" which he had committed against his Maker all year long.

The silence was broken when Rabbi Levi Yitzhak's lips stirred in a whisper: "I have come to stand and entreat before You for Your people Israel who have sent me …"

Suddenly, he stood up straight and began to recite his Kaddish, whose words and melody the tzaddik composed at that moment.

Thus sang Rabbi Levi Yitzhak: "Good morning to You, Master of the universe. I, Levi Yitzhak ben Sarah of Berdichev, come to stand before You in prayer, entreaty, and appeal. Tell me, Master of the universe, what is Your business with the People of Israel? Why did You impose Yourself specifically on them? In Your Torah, You wrote, 'Speak.' To whom are You speaking? To the People of Israel! You also wrote, 'Say.' To whom are You saying? Only to the People of Israel! You also wrote, 'Command.' Whom are You commanding? Again, the People of Israel!

"Compassionate and gracious Father, what do You want of the People of Israel? Are there not many nations in the world – Babylonians, Persians, Ishmaelites, Midianites? So why do You bother the People of Israel? Because Israel is beloved to You, and are called 'God's children.' So I shall ask You, Master of the universe, is this the way parents treat their children?

"Master of the world, look. There are English people in the world – what do they say? That their king is the greatest and strongest of all kings. There are French people in the world – what do they say? That their leader rules the world. And the Russians, what do they say? That their czar is the only ruler. And the Turks? That their sultan is sovereign over all.

"And I, Levi Yitzhak ben Sarah, say, '*Yitgadal veyitkadash shemeh rabba!*' – Magnified and sanctified is God's great name.

"I will not leave here; I will not move from this place; no, I will not move from this place until there be an end to the exile, until the days of the Messiah draw near, until all nations recognize this: '*Yitgadal veyitkadash shemeh rabba*' – Magnified and sanctified is God's great name!"

ﻙﻙﻙ

When Did the Tzaddik Smile?

Rabbi Levi Yitzhak of Berdichev was enveloped in grief and tension from the beginning of the recitation of *Kol Nidrei* on Yom Kippur eve until the middle of the *Ne'ila* prayer at the end of the sacred day.

But just before the conclusion of the repetition of the *Ne'ila* prayer, the face of the tzaddik suddenly lit up and a smile of joy and contentment spread across his face.

At the conclusion of the evening prayer and *Kiddush Levana*, Rabbi Levi Yitzhak chanted *Havdala* on a cup of wine with great enthusiasm, as he generally did. Then he turned to his Hasidim and said: "On this Yom Kippur, a terrible accusation against the Jewish people was made in heaven. It was as if an iron wall was erected, separating us from our Father in heaven. And toward evening, when the repetition of the *Ne'ila* prayer was almost finished, two women began to talk among themselves about matters at hand.

"One woman said to her friend, 'I have full confidence that through our prayers we have achieved a good, blessed year for all of the Jewish people.'

"'What is the source of this confidence?' asked her friend.

"'Can it be otherwise?' answered the first woman. 'Had we been standing, heaven forbid, in front of a thief and begun to plead and cry before him, even he would have taken pity on us!'"

Rabbi Levi Yitzhak paused for a moment in his explanation. He then continued:

"The few simple words that the woman said during the recitation of *Ne'ila* made an enormous impression on the upper worlds. And in that very moment, as if with a wave of the hand, the grave accusation which lay heavily on the heads of our brothers all during the hours of the holy day was lifted."

The Heavenly Tribunal

Rabbi Levi Yitzhak's students once entered their rabbi's room at the conclusion of Yom Kippur to see how he was faring after fasting and praying all day with deep fervor, as was his custom. The rabbi was seated at his desk, and even though several hours had already passed since the end of the fast, he still had not touched the cup of coffee in front of him.

When he saw his students he lifted his head and said: "It is good that you have come. I will explain what happened. You should know that Satan made an accusation before the tribunal on high and argued: 'You, members of the righteous tribunal, explain something to me. When a person steals a ruble from someone, you take into consideration the amount of money stolen in order to decide what punishment to mete out to the thief, and you do not take into consideration the people who stole the money. But when someone gives a ruble as charity, you take into consideration the poor person who receives the charity, and all the members of his family who benefit from the gift. Why do you not in this case, too, take into consideration the amount of money? Or why do you not take into consideration in the first case the person whose ruble was stolen, and his whole household, who suffered from the loss?'

"At that point," continued the rabbi, "I interrupted the proceedings and explained: 'The person giving charity wants to preserve the life of people. Therefore, the individuals are taken into consideration. But the thief wants only the money, and pays no mind to the people. Therefore, in such a case only the rubles are taken into consideration.' In this way I shut the mouth of Satan."

The next year, at the close of Yom Kippur, Rabbi Levi Yitzhak invited one of the successful business agents in the city to visit him.

"Are you a well-known expert as a middleman?" asked the rabbi.

"Yes, honorable rabbi," replied the agent. "Is this not my craft and my profession?"

"Did you ever have occasion to serve as middleman in a case where a large amount of money was involved, from which you received a large payment as your fee?"

"Yes," answered the mediator. "I closed several large deals and received thousands of rubles as my fee."

"If that is the case," said Rabbi Levi Yitzhak, "I request of you to decide what my fee from the Blessed Holy One should be when I mediated with Him. Today, I served as a mediator between

Him and the People of Israel, and I brought a large transaction to a successful conclusion. I turned to the Blessed One and told Him, 'Here in the lower world there are sins and transgressions. In Your upper world there is pardon, forgiveness, and atonement.' And an exchange was agreed upon. How much of a mediation fee should I collect?"

"Honorable rabbi," answered the mediator in surprise. "I am not an expert in matters of this nature, and I am not able to determine a proper fee for mediation in heaven."

"If so," said Rabbi Levi Yitzhak, "I will set the fee that I demand for this mediation: my children, my life, and my sustenance; a good life and a good living for all of the Jewish people. Is this not a fair request?"

ﾃﾞﾞﾞ

Creator of Living Beings

Rabbi Levi Yitzhak of Berdichev prayed all day on Yom Kippur with supreme effort.

Once, at the conclusion of Yom Kippur, the tzaddik fainted and no one could arouse him. They brought him an etrog, and when he smelled the fragrance of a mitzva, he immediately awakened.

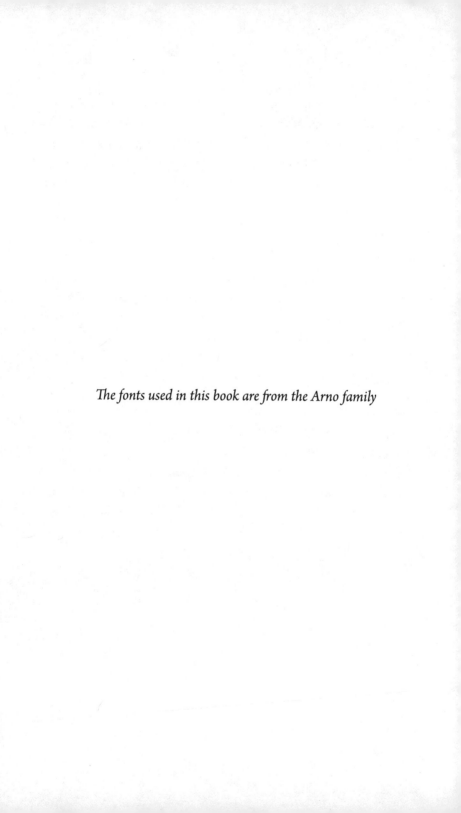

Menorah Books
At the Heart of Judaism